RED ROCK
STORIES

RED ROCK
STORIES

THREE GENERATIONS OF WRITERS
SPEAK ON BEHALF OF UTAH'S PUBLIC LANDS

EDITED BY STEPHEN TRIMBLE

TORREY HOUSE PRESS
SALT LAKE CITY · TORREY

First Torrey House Press Edition, April 2017
Copyright © 2017 by Torrey House Press

Published by Torrey House Press
Salt Lake City, Utah
www.torreyhouse.org

International Standard Book Number: 978-1-937226-79-4
E-book ISBN: 978-1-937226-80-0
Library of Congress Control Number: 2016943567
RED ROCK TESTIMONY chapbook design by Timothy Ross Lee
RED ROCK STORIES book design by Alisha Anderson

All royalties from RED ROCK STORIES
go to the Utah Wilderness Coalition, to fund grassroots
organizing on behalf of Utah's redrock wilderness.

TO THE NATIVE LEADERS OF THE
BEARS EARS INTER-TRIBAL COALITION

With graciousness and tenacity
you reminded us all of the meaning of sacred land.
In bringing Bears Ears National Monument
to the president, you created the healing and
reconciliation you sought.

CONTENTS

RED ROCK
STORIES

PREFACE:
WRITING INTO THE WHIRLWIND

In the utter simplicity of ink on paper, the writers in *Red Rock Stories* take readers deep into the wildness and restorative power of southern Utah's canyon country. These women and men have chosen to wield their words on behalf of this land, to counter those who see these canyons and mesas as nothing more than commodities to use and use up. And so when these storytellers evoke rivers running red in flood, when they summon the healing warmth of sun on stone, their words ring with both the solemnity of prayer and the fires of resistance.

In these pages you'll hear the glissade of a canyon wren's call breaking the stillness of a summer afternoon. You'll share in the writers' delight as they capture in language this place where, in Lauret Savoy's words, "aridity conspires with erosion to expose Earth's anatomy." You'll sense the ancient bonds to these mesas and mountains carried by Native peoples.

As readers, we understand how writing can transport us. I've sobbed at the endings of novels and memoirs. I've gasped and chortled and seethed with spitfire anger as I read strong non-fiction. I've melted at the perfectly chosen images in poems. And I've learned the language of every landscape I cherish from reading the writers who have made these places their home territories in life and work.

Words that grow from such deep roots can be contemplative and soothing, but *Red Rock Stories* means to raise the stakes. When politicians campaign to open up irreplaceable wildlands to destructive industry, when the white men in power scorn the traditional knowledge of Native elders and the sacred inheritance of ruins and rock art, when local officials disdain the shared national ownership of public lands, redrock writers move from quiet journaling to passionate advocacy.

We created this book to capture these emotions and deliver them to Washington, D.C.—and now, to you. The contributors write with purpose and urgency, a need even more pressing since the presidential election of 2016. These writers aim to inform you, to call you to action, to change your life, to create the future. They just may have influenced President Barack Obama when he created Bears Ears National Monument on December 28, 2016.

We'll need their message for years to come. The fossil fuel industry and its supporters in politics and the rural West never cease attacking, never relent in their crusade to wring maximum profit from public lands. We'll need inspiration as we rally again and again to oppose schemes to develop, fragment, sell, or diminish the redrock wilderness.

———————————————

Red Rock Stories grew organically from events at the beginning of 2016, when a confluence of hostilities and opportunities surfaced in western wildlands.

The whirlwind of threats ranged from sweeping demands for local control of public lands to Utah Republican congressional representatives Rob Bishop's and Jason Chaffetz's Public Lands Initiative. This legislation promised to address the big issues on federal lands in eastern Utah with a "grand compromise" supported by all. Instead, the PLI bill turned out to be both woefully inadequate as conservation and dangerously precedent-setting in promoting rampant fossil fuel extraction.

In response, the Salt Lake City writing community began to meet, called together by a couple of long-time activists—all of us ready to ally ourselves with the long tradition of writing in support of conservation.

We had one remarkable campaign to support, the unparalleled Bears Ears Inter-Tribal Coalition proposal. Five southwestern Native nations had asked President Obama to proclaim a national monument on 1.9 million acres in southeast Utah, to protect extraordinary sacred lands from archaeological vandalism and destructive energy development. The tribes asked for co-management of the Bears Ears, honoring traditional knowledge along with western science.

We asked, how can we best participate in these conversations and affect these decisions with our essays and poems and stories?

Our concerned group of citizen-writers had a powerful model, a 1995 book created at a similar moment of crisis, *Testimony: Writers of the West Speak on Behalf of Utah Wilderness.*

In the mid-1990s, Congress was considering a bill that would undermine the integrity of the 1964 Wilderness Act and open up millions of acres of Utah's public lands to devastating development. As colleagues and friends based in Salt Lake City, Terry Tempest Williams and I decided that our best chance to counter this anti-wilderness bill lay in gathering short pieces from twenty writers with deep ties to Utah wildlands. In just two months, we invited submissions, snagged a small grant to pay for printing, and took the compilation of writing to

Washington, D.C., where we delivered a copy of our chapbook to every member of Congress. We had no idea if the book would matter. We sent these pieces of writing into the offices of decision makers as an act of faith. But when Senators Bill Bradley (D-NJ) and Russ Feingold (D-WI) successfully led the filibuster that defeated the bill, they read essays from *Testimony* on the floor of the Senate. When President Bill Clinton proclaimed Grand Staircase-Escalante National Monument in 1996, he held up a copy of *Testimony* and said, "This made a difference."

" These writers aim to inform you, to call you to action, to change your life, to create the future.

And so, with this 2016 round of attacks on public lands—and the promise of the Bears Ears monument—the Utah writing community once again asked, do we need a *Testimony II*?

Kirsten Johanna Allen asked that question most forcefully and answered with a resounding "yes." She is both an ardent conservationist and advocate as well as publisher of Utah's nonprofit Torrey House Press. She asked me to edit and made the commitment to publish this trade edition after initial distribution of a chapbook in the circles of power in Washington, D.C. With a bow toward the original *Testimony*, we called our chapbook of essays and poems *Red Rock Testimony*. We call this expanded version you hold in your hands *Red Rock Stories*.

As we began work in April 2016, we invited nearly 60 writers with ties to Utah to contribute, reaching far beyond the concerned people gathered in Salt Lake City. Writers and citizens from every state love the southern Utah canyon country, and we wished to emphasize that universality. Charles Wilkinson, the preeminent Indian law scholar who was volunteering with the Bears Ears Inter-Tribal Coalition, helped us to reach out to Native writers, since the Bears Ears proposal owed so much to the sensibilities, traditions, and vision of the tribes. Charles begins the book with a quick survey of Colorado Plateau conservation that places the events of 2016 in context.

We gave writers little more than a month to deliver their manuscripts—leaving just enough time for printing before we took the book to Washington in mid-June. The invitees responded with extraordinary efforts, nearly all sending original work. Kathleen Dean Moore wrote her piece about the legacy we will leave to our children while she camped along the goosenecked canyons of the San Juan River during a five-day float trip. She fired off her draft the moment she reached cell service. Gary Nabhan wrote when pain from his recent knee surgery kept him awake in the middle of the night. He recalled a transformative backpacking trip into the Bears Ears as a young man, and I suspect that memory helped him to heal.

Contributors were gracious when we excerpted their longer pieces to make everything fit into 88 pages, the maximum length for a saddle-stitched chapbook. As essays and poems poured in, we realized that the birthdates of these writers ranged from Brooke Larsen, born in 1992, to Bruce Babbitt, born in 1938. Our subtitle became obvious: *Three Generations of Writers Speak on Behalf of Utah's Public Lands.*

With the printer racing to meet our deadline, in June 2016, Kirsten Allen and I took our cartons of books to Washington, D.C. We distributed copies to decision makers—to staffers at all levels in the land management agencies, to the President's Council on

Environmental Quality, and to a few key members of Congress. Shortly afterward, we sent the book to every member of Congress with a rousing cover letter from Bruce Babbitt.

We hope the book reached the hands and hearts of the Secretary of the Interior Sally Jewell and of President Barack Obama. We hope these words helped to inspire the president's decision to proclaim this innovative 1.35-million-acre national monument during his last month in office.

These writers make their homes from New England to California, from Oregon to North Carolina. About a dozen of our 35 contributors live in Utah. We've created a community chorus whose lives span nine decades, a montage of poems and essays that includes Native and Hispanic voices, warnings from elders and challenges from millennials, personal emotional journeys, and lyrical nature writing. These pieces address historical context, natural history and archaeology, energy threats, faith, and politics. Together, they offer a nuanced case for restraint and respect in this incomparable redrock landscape.

In *Red Rock Stories*, the essays and poems we shortened for *Red Rock Testimony* have the freedom to expand to their full length, to breathe freely. We have also included a "Red Rock History" postscript, archiving the documents that led to this book and to the Bears Ears proclamation.

The contributors to *Red Rock Stories* speak as individuals, with untethered artistic freedom. They ask to be heard as writers, as citizens, honoring the land without ties to any single advocacy organization. We include no photographs, no art. We have faith in the abilities of these poets, journalists, and essayists to nourish and embolden readers with only their words.

We send these pieces on their way and believe that here and there a congressional staffer, a BLM administrator holed up in a stuffy office, or a citizen activist in love with redrock wilderness may pick up the book and start leafing through the pages. They'll find a moment of respite and a sense of pride, for these writers honor the good work of these officials and advocates and celebrate the places they labor to protect.

Perhaps Alastair Bitsoi catches that reader's eye when he says, "Bears Ears will always be a significant healing space for young Navajos like me, who live in the concrete jungle that is New York City." Maybe another reader lands on Regina Lopez-Whiteskunk being "floored by the amount of disrespect" she received when the chair of a legislative hearing at the Utah Capitol rudely cut her off as she spoke of the "personal healing like nothing else" that she finds in the Bears Ears.

We offer many ways into the argument for protecting these endangered lands. Mary Sojourner tells of meeting a guy named Bear Campbell in a Flagstaff bar and going camping with him in the woods below Bears Ears. Anne Terashima writes as a millennial grateful for time on the Green River in Labyrinth Canyon, a chance to disconnect from Instagram and Facebook. David Gessner ponders the "freedom of restraint" and concludes that "here freedom becomes more than a jingoistic word used to wage war and sell trucks." And Bruce Babbitt, who served as Secretary of the Interior under President Bill Clinton, makes the case for Bears Ears as a former Arizona attorney general and president of the League of Conservation Voters: "The best way to defend the Antiquities Act is for the President to use it."

––––––––––––––––

With the transition to an administration led by Republicans who abhor such bold acts of conservation and who have little inter-est in acknowledging Native people, we know these *Red Rock Stories* matter more than ever. Perhaps Senators Dick Durbin (D-IL) or Martin Heinrich (D-NM) or Congressman Alan Lowenthal

(D-CA)—all champions of southern Utah public lands—will find words here even yet, to use when it comes time to lead the fight against bad legislation or to counter renewed attacks on the Antiquities Act.

We know we'll be fighting on behalf of the land during the next four years and for the rest of our lives. We know that much of what these writers have to say applies to landscapes far beyond Utah. And so *Red Rock Stories* has a long life.

When politics and advocacy grow exhausting and discouraging, turn to these stories from the redrock for rekindling and refuge. We'll need these writers' eloquent calls for protection of the Colorado Plateau now and forever.

As *Red Rock Stories* went to press, while polls in Indian Country and across the West documented overwhelming support of Bears Ears and national monument designations, Utah's elected officials thundered their demands to rescind Bears Ears National Monument. In response, Simon Ortiz reassured the redrock writing community—and all of us—with these wise words:

"Our belief in our community—human, animal, plant, desert, mountain, stars above—will prevail and sustain us.

"Now we know what we must do, a line from a Pueblo song. The land shall endure. There will be victory. The land will go on. We shall have victory."

STEPHEN TRIMBLE
Salt Lake City, February 2017

" When politics and advocacy grow exhausting and discouraging, turn to these stories from the redrock for rekindling and refuge. "

The Holy People lived here in the beginning.
They built the first hooghan, made the first weapon
sang the first songs and made the first prayers.

Diné language, ceremonies,
history, and beliefs began here.
This is where we began.

Luci Japahonso

LUCI TAPAHONSO
b. 1953

11

INTRODUCTION:
LISTENING TO THE OLD PEOPLE,
THE LAND, AND THE LONG FUTURE

he Canyon Country—in the Four Corners states of Utah, Arizona, New Mexico, and Colorado—can make us shout out in excitement but, even more fundamentally, it is a place that slows us down and inspires our contemplation, reflection, and wonderment.

How do the plants in this rocky, arid landscape make it? How long did it take to make that hole, that arch, across the way? All the other impossible red rock formations, how were they made? Out on the tip of a mesa, how far am I seeing? Eighty miles? A hundred? More? Down in the redrock side canyons I find inspiring villages, granaries, kivas, and petroglyphs and pictographs left by the Old People—the Ancestral Puebloans. Those societies were there for thousands of years. How could they have made it for so long in this unforgiving setting?

While more needs to be done, large expanses of the Canyon Country land have been protected. The Canyon Country holds world-renowned national parks, among them Arches, Canyonlands, Capitol Reef, Monument Valley, Zion, and the Grand Canyon itself— all federal public land, open to all. This is the largest concentration of parks and monuments in the world, mostly a result of the

Antiquities Act of 1906, when Congress granted presidents the unilateral right to create national monuments with a stroke of a pen.

The Antiquities Act quickly took root in the Canyon Country. In 1908, Theodore Roosevelt came to the Grand Canyon and declared that 800,000 acres would become the Grand Canyon National Monument. "Let this great wonder of nature remain as it now is," the president exhorted from the South Rim. "You cannot improve on it." Ever since, the Antiquities Act has remained a foundation stone of American conservation policy.

After World War II, interest in the Canyon Country accelerated. Congress made Canyonlands a national park in 1964. Capitol Reef and Arches, both originally created as national monuments, became national parks in 1971. Glen Canyon National Recreation Area was established in 1972. Several smaller units were named. Disagreements over these measures were mild.

Then Utah political leaders blasted apart the tradition of good civil discourse and made the topic of conservation ugly, toxic. The cause for this? Just a mild initiative in the 1976 Bureau of Land Management Organic Act calling for a study of BLM roadless areas for wilderness study. No wilderness was created. It was just a study.

Southern Utah frothed at the mouth when the study areas were announced in the summer of 1979. In Moab, for example, on July Fourth the city fathers fired up bulldozers, draped them with American flags, and bulldozed the barriers at the heads of Negro Bill Canyon and Mill Creek Canyon. They charged on, gashing "roads" deep into the pristine canyons. Illegal conduct and abuse of the land became accepted conduct. No matter how glorious the land in question, "wilderness," "conservation," and "environmentalism" were fighting words.

The anger and resistance burns today. To be sure, it has leavened somewhat in southern Utah, and broadly so in the state at large, as long-time residents see the benefits of protected lands. New arrivals came for the call of the land and acknowledge that the economy is built on recreation. Hardly a hammer hits a nail in southern Utah for any other economic reason.

Still, for complex reasons of history, habit, and hard-headedness, official Utah—the congressional delegation, the governors, most of the state legislature, and county commissioners—remains bound to the old clenched-fist conviction that all conservation is wrong and that unfettered mining and ranching is right.

So the real imperatives of the present and future have gathered maturity and authority. The conservation community has expanded and deepened. The tribes, kept down for so long, have built an historic revival nationally, west-wide, and in Utah. Three generations ago, they were hanging on, groups with little authority in the outside world. Today, they embody Chief Justice John Marshall's accurate acknowledgment of them as sovereign nations. They are full-service governments with hundreds of employees or more and charged by a burning determination to be rare societies resting on pillars of both authentic traditionalism and modernism. The millennial-old respect and knowledge of, and union with, the land is undeniable. "We aren't," their tribal leaders make clear, "going anywhere."

───────────────

All of this plays out at Bears Ears, a distinctive formation of twin buttes rising high above the piñon-juniper forests of Cedar Mesa. If you know Cedar Mesa, you *feel* the many curvy canyons cutting down each side, redrock canyons so wild and exquisite, and so rich with the work of the Old People, that they leave you with no adequate words. Numerous tribes are deeply connected to this landscape. For them, it is a place for healing.

In 2010, Utah Diné Bikéyah, a nonprofit organization of Navajos, Utes, and other tribes, began documenting the facts necessary to get the greater Bears Ears area protected. They built an extraordinary historical record of the land that the military had force-marched them off in the mid-1800s. They put together oral histories, cultural maps, and multi-layer analyses of sacred sites, archaeological locations of the Old People, gathering areas, wildlife habitats, mineral deposits, creeks, and springs. That led them to identifying boundaries, encompassing 1.9 million acres of federal public land, and a strategy for protecting it—a national monument under the Antiquities Act.

The chances of success received a dramatic boost in 2014, when word came out of Washington, D.C. that President Obama wanted to use this great statute in a way no president had ever done—to honor diversity, that is, the work of minorities, of dispossessed peoples.

From then on, events moved quickly and on July 15, 2015, the pieces fell into place at a memorable meeting in Towaoc, Colorado, the governmental seat of the Ute Mountain Ute tribe. This was a large gathering of tribal governmental leaders, medicine men, tribal professionals, and other Indian people committed to the culture and the land.

A central question involved leadership. Utah Diné Bikéyah had always recognized that, as a nonprofit, they could not carry out the project to protect Bears Ears alone. The sovereign tribal nations had to do that. It was agreed that the five tribes with the deepest connections to Bears Ears—the Hopi, Navajo, Uintah and Ouray Ute, Ute Mountain Ute, and Zuni—would lead the effort to obtain a presidential proclamation under the Antiquities Act. By consensus, the group formally established the Bears Ears Inter-Tribal Coalition. The other tribes of the Southwest soon announced support of the Coalition, as did the National Congress of American Indians.

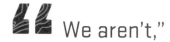 We aren't,"

tribal leaders make clear,

"going anywhere."

At the meeting, the tribes also resolved to present President Obama with a comprehensive proposal for a Bears Ears National Monument in just three months, no later than October 15, 2015. They knew that time was short. President Obama would be leaving office in January 2017.

For my part, although I had been working on Native American and federal public land issues for forty-five years, this was my first meeting on Bears Ears. Yet the authenticity, passion, and rightness of it hit me in a way that few projects ever have. Late in the meeting, I found myself, unasked, promising to commit as many hours of my services as an unpaid volunteer as would be necessary. Even as I spoke, because I could see how much work lay ahead, I wondered if it would prove to be too much of a commitment. It has not. Leaving aside my family, I've never made a better decision.

With the Coalition a welcomed and vibrant force from the beginning, and with people with diverse talents rushing in on a volunteer basis, things moved quickly. The Coalition filed its comprehensive proposal with President Obama, as they had promised, on October 15, 2015.

The historic nature of the proposal is unprecedented. Until now, requests for presidential action under the Antiquities Act have always come from the conservation community. The Bears Ears proposal is the first submitted by Indian tribes. The conservation community broadly supports the Coalition's proposal.

The Bears Ears proposal, if put into place, would mark the first time that tribes have worked with federal officials to operate a public lands unit under tribal-federal collaborative management. Unquestionably, modern Indian tribes have the capacity to take on the task. Tribal leaders are confident to a certainty that this will lead to more sensitive and holistic protection of the Bears Ears landscape.

The Obama administration, while acknowledging the force of the Coalition proposal, asked the tribes to seek a legislative resolution in Congress before relying on the Antiquities Act. The potential vehicle was the Public Lands Initiative, which two congressmen were developing to resolve Utah conservation issues raging for decades.

The tribes did engage with the PLI effort. Still, the ossified Utah view of public land protection made progress impossible. The PLI was a ruse. Although they never said it, the Utah delegation clearly believed that intensive resource development, especially mining, always trumps land protection. Tribal leaders knew they were not being truly listened to or respected. On December 31, 2015, they were forced, as both dreamers and practical people, to withdraw from the PLI and place their hopes with President Obama and the Antiquities Act, where they are optimistic that the best visions of the Old People and the modern-yet-traditional people of today can be realized.

President Obama will leave office on January 20, 2017, so the days are few to make complete a statement that is eternal in that it both reaches farther back into time than we can conceive and will stand for more time into the future than we can imagine.

CHARLES WILKINSON
b. 1941

RIGHT OF WAY

The elder people at home do not understand.
It is hard to explain to them.
The questions from their mouths
and on their faces are unanswerable.
You tell them, "The State wants right of way.
It will get right of way."

They ask, "What is right of way?"
You say, "The State wants to go through
your land. The State wants your land."
They ask, "The Americans want my land?"
You say, "Yes, my beloved Grandfather."
They say, "I already gave them some land."
You say, "Yes, Grandmother, that's true.
Now, they want more, to widen their highway."
They ask again and again, "This right of way
that the Americans want, does that mean
they want all our land?"

There is silence.
There is silence.
There is silence because you can't explain,
and you don't want to, and you know
when you use words like industry
and development and corporations
it wouldn't do any good.

There is silence.
There is silence.
You don't like to think
the fall into a bottomless despair
is too near and too easy and meaningless.
You don't want that silence to grow
deeper and deeper into you
because that growth inward stunts you,
and that is no way to continue,
and you want to continue.

And so you tell stories.
You tell stories about your People's birth
and their growing.
You tell stories about your children's birth
and their growing.
You tell the stories of their struggles.
You tell that kind of history,
and you pray and be humble.
With strength, it will continue that way.
That is the only way.
That is the only way.

SIMON ORTIZ
b. 1941

" It's impossible to separate the need for wildness from the need for climate justice. "

THE EYES OF THE YOUNG

As I descend the sticky sandstone cliffs into the Dirty Devil wilderness, anxiety seeps over me. Heading into the backcountry for three days makes me stop and run through any unsent emails before leaving cell service behind. I feel an unease in disconnecting from technology that overshadows my relief in reconnecting with nature. But as a child of the redrock, that feeling quickly fades. My jaw loosens, my eyes come alive, and I howl. I hear the echo as a reminder that I am untamable.

I am in my early twenties. My generation is screen saturated and nature deprived. We find constant connection in our digital world, yet we hunger for depth. Our friendships grow in quantity rather than quality. Our relationship with ourselves and our environment degrades as our fear of solitude and silence grows. It's not revolutionary to say my generation needs wildness more than ever.

I reach the Dirty Devil and sink my feet in the mud at the river's edge. Joy tingles every inch of my flesh, awakening my wild spirit. For me, few things match the beauty and awe of flowing water in a landscape of red. Even the rivers run red. One could say this landscape is parched earth, but as long as rivers flow, life seems in perfect balance. If I have children, will they also find a flowing Dirty Devil in fifty years?

The forces trying to desecrate this landscape leave more than initial scars, schisms, and spills. The oil rigs and natural gas flares contribute to a much more existential threat—climate change. For my generation, it's impossible to separate the need for wildness from the need for climate justice. Protecting this landscape is not just protecting our human spirit—it's protecting the future of all life in the region. With daunting climate change projections, it's realistic to wonder if the Dirty Devil will still flow for the next generation. The economic, legal and biological ramifications of a water-stressed Colorado River Basin are well known. But what about the spiritual?

Crossing the Dirty Devil River, I head towards the canyons of the Robbers Roost. In popular culture, Robbers Roost is known as the outlaw hideout of Butch Cassidy and the Sundance Kid. For desert dwellers, it's known for its wildness. Here, I follow coyote tracks rather than human footprints. I respect the power of water and wind to carve stories into walls. I experience desperately needed solitude and silence.

The redrock is my teacher of humility. In a society where young people can navigate anywhere with an app, I learn from navigating based on geologic layers and topographic lines. In a culture where we can have food delivered to us in minutes, I learn from planning my survival around the dependability of perennial streams.

> "The eyes of young people are closely watching. The spirits of future generations are pleading."

We realize our own insignificance. We realize our vulnerability.

My family has called Utah home for six generations, but unlike most Utahns, I didn't grow up with religion. I grew up questioning. My story is written in carved slot canyons and desert washes. Wildness became my spiritual refuge—particularly the redrock wilderness of southern Utah. So if I respect the churches of others, why are the leaders of my state constantly disrespecting mine? Protecting the redrock is self-preservation.

The red earth is bleeding. How many more cuts will it endure? Each drop of oil extracted matches the tears that will flow when this region is no longer livable. The deep time of the redrock inspires hope—from the geologic story told in layers of orange, pink and red to the rock art left by ancestors of Native Americans who still call Bears Ears home. However, it increasingly feels like we are running out of time.

The eyes of young people are closely watching. The spirits of future generations are pleading. We must hear these pleas and rise. Elected leaders will come and go, but redrock devotees will never fade. Through shared love of red earth, we will build community in unlikely places with power to resist taming and courage to howl louder. Walking hand in hand, the redrock is our guide.

BROOKE LARSEN
b. 1992

UNTHINKABLE

I am an old-timer in a "new west." I have lived, taught, loved and fought in this beautiful landscape for five decades. But sometimes I feel as though I am a hundred years old and dragging an anchor through my ancient and worthy western landscape with a bowed head and aching back, facing yet more conflict with people who do not and perhaps cannot understand the deep meaning and salvation to be found in wild lands. It has been a long uphill battle to have my wild spaces recognized for their intrinsic worth, not simply economic value. And the battle is far from over.

The redrock and mountainous west is my home, my passion, the seat of my soul. I intend to work on behalf of this landscape for as long as I am alive and able. I want my children and their children and generations beyond to see and enjoy what I have seen. To go where I have gone. To know what I know. There is no place on Earth like this wild western country. It is our duty to do everything we can to protect this sacred land.

This "new west" is a place of greed, destruction, and ill concern. The fossil fuel and other extraction industries care nothing for the land or the people of the land. Their god is money; they are rapacious and soulless. Their goal is to feed the beast at any cost. They will destroy the Earth.

The redrock is my home,

my passion, the seat of my soul.

We currently have before us two of the most onerous and dangerous threats to Utah's lands ever to emerge. The first is a Public Lands Initiative introduced in 2016 by Utah Congressman Rob Bishop, who calls his proposal the "Grand Bargain." If you are in an extractive industry like grazing, mining or oil, the proposal is indeed a helluva Grand Bargain. You get nearly everything you could possibly ask, including reduced oversight and regulation, easier permitting, watershed devaluation, even airshed degradation in some national parks.

Many are calling Bishop's proposal a "fossil fuel development bill" or a "public lands giveaway initiative." It is both. This proposal benefits only those profiting from public lands. It gives scant protection to the wild lands that are our heritage. We the public must do everything we can to avert this disastrous initiative.

These are our lands. They are native lands. They do not belong to politicians to dole out as they see fit. They do not belong to the grazers or to extractive industries that are already privileged and allowed to use public lands at highly discounted costs to our ecosystems. For a century and a half, these public land users have destroyed our air and watersheds. They have ruined our grazing lands. They have caused land and soil erosion on a massive scale. Bishop's proposal allows more overuse and destruction of these lands. Approving this legislation is simply unthinkable if we want a sustainable Earth.

The second threat to Utah's public lands is even worse. This nefarious move comes from Utah Governor Gary Herbert and the GOP members of the Utah Legislature, who propose to "take back Utah's public lands from the federal government." How ironic. How is it possible to take back lands in Utah that were never owned by the state in the first place? This is mean-spirited propaganda aimed at the uninformed.

The GOP-dominated Utah state legislature and the governor have set aside millions of dollars for a frivolous lawsuit against the federal government to wrest public lands from we the people. But public lands are exactly that. They are lands owned by the public and used by the public for a multitude of purposes under the oversight of federal land managers. This partnership between agencies and the public has been successful. Those opposed want control of these lands without oversight. They advocate the purchase of these public lands for private use and profit, which can only lead to the despoiling of our lands by dirty unsustainable energy.

My children, my spouse and I have seen close-up the west we love. We have hiked, biked, and skied the majestic peaks of the Wasatch, the La Sals, the Abajos, Navajo Mountain, and so many others without intrusive clear-cuts, over-grazed meadows, "sheep-burn," polluted, trampled and eroded streams, and sullied air. We have walked the splendid wild areas and national parks of our canyon country without oil pumpers, gas pads, the permanent scars of operational and abandoned mines, and the hundreds of roads to service these sites. We have seen the bright night skies of some of the darkest places on Earth. We have worshipped the land and thrived on the sustenance that has helped us grow into better people and better stewards of an Earth we have borrowed from the future. We have benefitted immeasurably by our emotional attachment to these wild and sacred lands.

So beware Utah citizens and all Americans. These proposals, the Bishop Public Lands Initiative and the Utah Public Land Grab and others like them, are coming to a political venue or a courtroom near you. We must be vigilant. We must insist on transparency. We must seek clean air and drinkable water and wild lands. Beware of those who would rob you of your heritage, degrade Earth, and make a future for coming generations far poorer than they deserve.

SAM RUSHFORTH
b. 1945

I've been floating all week in Desolation
Between the Tavaputs and the reservation
I talked to the man with a heart of stone
Standing on the wall of time.

I've been hot, I've been cold, I've had every sensation
To me it's more than recreation
I've been to a place where time stands still
It brings me peace of mind.

—from the song ANCIENT PLACES
by Kevin T. Jones

THE MAN WITH A HEART OF STONE

There's a place in Desolation Canyon where a figure stands out, perhaps only to me, on a sandstone monolith covered with petroglyphs. An anthropomorph whose head is haloed by an array of dots, whose torso is pecked solid save for one spot in the center of his chest, and two where his testicles would be. A nearby figure in the same style depicts a female whose breasts are likewise highlighted. Each time I see this couple my surroundings rush away as though I am hurtling through time, entering hyperspace, and I am immersed in, and part of, this wall of time.

The man with a heart of stone has adorned the canyon for at least five hundred years, perhaps much longer. How many others has he beckoned, how many others have relinquished the present to vault lightspeeding through time-space as they stood transfixed in the very spot where so long ago an outstanding artist altered this stone in a way that speaks across centuries? Across cultures, across languages and beliefs, he speaks in a complete and universal way, the language of humanity. And he speaks directly to me, seemingly to me alone.

He shows as much as speaks. He shows me a long view of time. He has stood in that same place since before machines and moon landings and missiles, and will be there when an unimaginably different future flows by, and then some. My conversation with him centers me in time.

Desolation Canyon is a strip of wilderness, some even designated as such. We may think of wilderness as untouched by humans, but that is a very ethnocentric view. Over the millennia, native people have been through and over every square inch of this land. They have been intimate with it. The traces the ancient ones left may be subtle, but they are there, and they speak to us.

Each time a new something is imposed on the land, it erases the traces of those who came before.

The man with a heart of stone and his companion were incised by a master stonecarver of what we call today the Fremont Culture, which flourished all across this region for nearly a thousand years. From what is now Cedar City to Vernal, Green River to Brigham City and beyond, the Fremont people were farmers, builders, dreamers, and thinkers, and they mastered the art of living in this harsh land, occupying and thriving and decorating the canyon walls with their mysterious, evocative images.

Climate change rocked the stone foundations of the Fremont Culture. To the south, the related

Anasazi were torn asunder, as were farming communities and emerging civilizations all across North America. Economies collapsed and social organization fell into chaos. As their farms failed and cultural institutions crumbled, the Fremont disappeared from the archaeological record in all but the deep clefts in the Colorado Plateau in the northeastern part of the Fremont world, including Desolation Canyon. The last refuge of the once vast Fremont empire appears to have been in the vicinity of the man with a heart of stone.

Modern Europeans have spent a mere few hundred years or so in the American West, but they have left their marks nearly everywhere, and the gouges are not subtle. Roads, dams, bridges, wells, mines, trails and structures mark the progress of the modern world, and they are nearly everywhere. Each time a new something is imposed on the land, it erases the traces of those who came before. It muffles the softly spoken universal tongue that can so powerfully penetrate the ages. It crushes the walls of time and topples them.

Desolation Canyon, a sanctuary for the ancient ones, is under assault. Oil and natural gas, tar sands, oil shale and who knows what lucre will lure another generation of boom and bust profiteers to the shores of the Green River, ready to pierce and tear at the earth, to rip the heart from the man of stone.

Why is the last refuge of the Fremont important? Where else can we learn about how climate change affected a thriving culture? Where else do traces of the past beckon us to investigate, examine, see? Where else can we stand at the wall of time and learn from a man with a heart of stone? Where else does time stand still?

KEVIN T. JONES
b. 1951

THE LAND OF NO USE

I f you drive into my town from the west, you will be guided by Powell Point, a 10,000-foot-high, jagged hunk of pink, red, lavender, or orange limestone—depending on the passing clouds and changing light—with a rim of white around its peak from which you can look down upon "The Blues," rolling hills of shale deposited eighty million years ago by an inland ocean.

From the east, you will travel The Hogsback, a suitably named narrow strip of pavement slapped down on an equally thin ribbon of rock. On either side, the earth abruptly spills to slickrock canyons below. The canyons tease with winding slivers of greenery, but they don't reveal their secrets: creeks and waterfalls and swimming holes, Fremont Indian art panels and ruins, dinosaur bones, songbirds and wild turkeys and mountain lions, sandy washes and red-walled slots.

No matter the direction, when you drive across the land to get to Escalante, Utah, you must acknowledge the exposed and ancient vulnerability of the earth; you must recognize the authority of wind and water and time; you must concede human lowliness. Or you must narrow the scope of your mind to prohibit such thoughts.

In 1948, the American psychologist Edward Tolman developed the hypothesis of "cognitive maps." Some of us, Tolman posited, develop "narrow strip maps," and others develop "broad compre-

Left alone, this land has the capacity to ignite a profound **"** shift in consciousness.

hensive maps," both of which operate literally and figuratively. Our external geography informs our internal geography.

Escalante is a narrow strip map of a town. In many ways, that defines much of Utah's cognitive map. In 1996, when President Clinton took the courageous step of designating Grand Staircase-Escalante National Monument, a slogan began showing up on the bumpers of pickup trucks in Escalante: *Wilderness: The Land of No Use.* My congress members, the authors of the Utah Public Lands Initiative, demand "long-term land use certainty." They make this demand on my behalf, for the benefit of rural communities like mine. They peddle the protection of culture and custom like snake oil. But that's my culture and custom they are hawking. I am sixth-generation Utahn, the daughter of a Utah cattle rancher and the granddaughter of a Utah sheepherder. And I'm not buying it.

I venture often into what my neighbors consider the land of no use. Whenever I find myself lunging for the next paycheck, whenever I'm knocked off balance because my computer and modem are not properly mating, I seek a soaring red wall streaked with desert varnish and painted with ancient figures. There, I settle myself into stillness and breathe slowly. The wonder of such a place is its indifference to my pain, my fear, my trials, my prerequisites. Such indifference is a gift, a teacher. Without it, we believe ourselves to be the center of the universe, a conviction that is proving embarrassingly wide of the mark.

W.H. Auden said, "We are lived by the powers

we pretend to understand." Sitting still in what remains of wilderness is as close as I, up against the limitations of my human mind, will ever get to understanding the powers that live me. Whether or not we choose to acknowledge it, humans have a soulful yearning for wildness. It is our nature. It embodies us firmly in place and allows us to love deeply, celebrate life, and know gratitude.

We have sacrificed much in our zeal to use the land.

We have sacrificed the instinctive human, the natural human, the animal human. In doing so, we have sanctioned a painfully slow and ugly death for ourselves. And there's some part of each one of us that knows the truth of this.

I fear that we are several generations past the human animal now—a fact that some find comforting. I do not. There are many arguments for leaving the fossiliferous and historically significant public lands of Utah undisturbed. But I am arguing for their protection on a level that cannot be measured in scholarly study, in scientific findings, in dinosaur bones, in dollars, in jobs, or in uses. I'm arguing for something that cannot be measured by any standard generally accepted in our society. Left alone, this land has the capacity to ignite a profound shift in consciousness, has the ability to locate immediate knowledge in the gut. There are few places left in the United States holding on to that sort of potency, and we desperately need them.

Let us please, for once in our lives, leave something alone and see if we can't find some human value in that. Let this land be that one experiment in human restraint, and let's see if we can't recapture a little dignity, a little humility, and maybe even a little humanity in the process.

JANA RICHMAN
b. 1956

THE FREEDOM OF RESTRAINT

remember the moment exactly and I remember the word that came with the moment. The word that the moment all but summoned:

Freedom.

For me, for many Americans, it is a word that has had any true meaning hammered out of it by rhetoric and commercialism. It has been worn down and out by too many truck commercials and blowhard politicians, a fine and shining word now left behind on the ground like an old soda can.

But now *freedom* was back-filling my mind.

It wasn't a bomb bursting in air that revived the word for me, but falling water. The rain had come down in Utah's redrock desert, an event made even more beautiful by rarity, a thing I had been waiting all week for, praying for, really, and now here it was sliding down the rock chutes that other summer rains had created over eons. I stared up at a huge sandstone chute, fifty feet above me, which, during the rains, served as a water slide. At the foot of the chute was a slimy pool from remnant rains. Ferns bearded its edge, hanging down, green against red. Water landed on rock with a ferocious splatter, shaking the maidenhair ferns, the

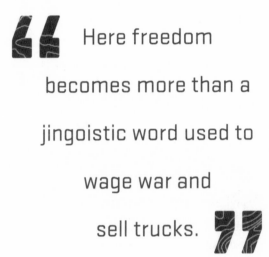 Here freedom becomes more than a jingoistic word used to wage war and sell trucks.

hackberry and buffaloberry plants, and splashing between two scrub oaks, a whole tiny oasis that had grown up here just for occasions like this. I ducked my head under the water and soaked myself and I started laughing.

I can't pretend my first thoughts at that moment were of grand ideals. I was filled with a giddy wild happiness, a sense of being unrestrained, a feeling that it was good to be an animal on planet earth. It wasn't until later, sitting around the fire, that my mind expanded with the night. I thought about how smart, how wise, our forebears had been to have the foresight to claim a place like this, not for any individual or corporation's profit, but for all of us, every American.

It's possible that my sense of intoxication was due to the beer I was drinking, but I don't think so. I think it was due to understanding, for the first time, what a stroke of genius putting aside land like this had been, and that the day I had just experienced, the wild freedom of it, had been the consequence of others coming before me not doing something.

The myths of western land are myths of freedom. Wallace Stegner wrote: "Lawlessness, like wildness, is attractive, and we conceive the last remaining home of both to be in the West." Yes: we come to places like this for that feeling of wildness, of lawlessness, the sense that we can do what we want and do it on our own. Those who want to take public land out of our hands, out of the people's hands, pepper their sentences with images of throwing off the shackles of the federal government and taking back their land. This is freedom of a sort but it is freedom for the few, impinging on the freedom of the many.

Championing restraint will never be as sexy as championing its opposite. But what I felt that day, under the water and later around the fire, was what I can only call the thrill of restraint, the excitement of it. Putting land aside for parks was, to paraphrase Stegner paraphrasing Lord Bryce, the best idea our country ever had. Quiet recreation—mountain biking, hiking, river rafting, backpacking, fishing, even, relatively speaking, hunting—brings almost a billion dollars into Utah each year, but what is gained goes far beyond the monetary. We define ourselves by our decision to keep land open to all. We say, "We are not chattel; we are not slaves; we do not make our every decision serve the powerful and ever-grinding economic machine." We say, in short, *we are free.*

This is what I thought sitting in front of the fire: the best thing about being an American is having places like this. Here freedom becomes more than a jingoistic word used to wage war and sell trucks. And if we let these places of freedom get swallowed up they are not coming back, and those who come after us, playing on their futuristic screens and looking at some virtual image of a waterfall splattering on redrock, will never know the feelings we felt. That is the irony of freedom. The only way for others, for our children and grandchildren, to experience the crazy, gleeful, youthful, mad feeling that I experienced, is if we are calm, restrained, and wise. This is a grown up version of freedom. This is the freedom of restraint.

DAVID GESSNER
b. 1961

THE ONLY WAY FORWARD

What you see depends on where you sit. I've been a mother, a teacher, a business owner, a writer, an activist, and a politician, and I can see things from many different points of view. My political experience tells me the decision about Bears Ears National Monument is beyond the ability of Utah's leaders to handle well. It can only be made by Executive Order of the President. Here's why:

The first people on this land we are fighting over were an ancient people. Wherever they lived, they honored the land like a parent honors a child. The idea of owning land was not in their vocabulary; as long as the land supported the plants and animals they needed to live, their lives were good. If they abused the land, it became worthless and they could not thrive. Even now, pushed onto reservations, they honor the land around them. In homes and trading posts I have visited, I have often seen tattered signs: "We don't inherit the earth. We borrow it from our children."

We the people who conquered the land and conquered the people who lived on the land think differently about the future. We talk of land use and land ownership. The elected state and national officials in Utah (according to polls, not necessarily representing the will of the people of Utah) demand the right to own and use the land that falls within the proposed Bears Ears National Monument.

Part of that land is also included in the Public Lands Initiative being forwarded in Congress by the Utah delegation, led by Representatives Rob Bishop and Jason Chaffetz. This bill is their answer to Utah's forty-year attempt to come to agreement on a Utah wilderness bill, although politics forbids the use of the word "wilderness" so the bill is the Public Lands Initiative or PLI.

Most of the Bears Ears area is excluded from the land the PLI protects as wilderness, and included parts are poorly protected. First, the bill weakens standing air quality requirements and permits the paving of dirt roads that are often only cow paths and may run near sacred ancient ruins. Second, a long section of the San Juan River that runs through the Bears Ears would become a fossil fuel zone and the bill makes clear that carbon development in the area covered by the bill takes precedence. *Use* of the land is the highest priority of Utah's elected officials.

The word that most often follows use is "up" as in *use up*. It's not always said aloud and that meaning is often denied. Frequently after whatever has been used up is gone, there are great exclamations

This fight is insolvable in Utah. If the Bears Ears is to be saved for our children, President Obama must save it.

47

of surprise and even regret, but then everyone gets used to the loss and goes on. That's what we the people do. We use up the things we own, taking it for granted they were there to be used up. Certainly that is the view of Utah's current political leaders. That is the basis of the fight over Bears Ears.

The chances that Native American voices can be heard here are remote. The Utah Diné Bikéyah has worked for many years to make this a conservation area and supports the monument. According to Utah Diné Bikéyah outreach director Cynthia Wilson, six of seven Navajo chapter houses in Utah have endorsed the Bears Ears Monument. When these people gathered at the Utah Capitol in April 2016 to speak at a hearing of the Commission for the Stewardship of Public Lands, they were told by Representative Mike Noel they were "selfish and greedy" for wanting to preserve the land. The co-chairwoman of the Bears Ears Inter-Tribal Coalition and head councilwoman of the Ute Mountain Ute Tribe, Regina Lopez-Whiteskunk, spoke with passion about efforts her group had made in past years to "reach across reservation and state boundary lines and other unwritten lines between one another," to bring Navajo and Ute views together. Her testimony was rudely interrupted again and again by Senator David Hinkins, R. Orangeville, who virtually ignored her answers and wanted to know why a male tribal representative was not there to testify.

For the others who spoke with passion about the need to protect the land around Cedar Mesa, where thousands of archaeological sites are now being pillaged and damaged, and for those who talked about how the land in the Abajo Mountains is sacred to them, a place they go to gather herbs and firewood and pursue spiritual experiences, there was hardly recognition. Their voices were not heard.

Representative Noel is presently conducting an investigation into the funding of the Utah Diné Bikéyah, which he suspects of being a front for Utah environmental groups.

This fight is insolvable in Utah. If the Bears Ears is to be saved for our children, President Obama must save it. It's the only way forward.

KAREN SHEPHERD
b. 1940

IT'S TIME TO HEAL BEARS EARS

I n the past, policies and laws have always been written as prescriptions for us Native American people to follow, including protecting the lands, dwellings, art, and final resting places of our ancestors. But now, for the first time, Native American people are using the law of the United States—the Antiquities Act of 1906—to ask the president of the United States to protect our cultural and spiritual homeland: an area we call the "Bears Ears" in southeastern Utah.

Our elders have called for the Bears Ears, which sheltered our ancestors for thousands of years, to be protected, not only for us, but for all people. And our leaders have listened to this people's movement. A coalition of sovereign nations: the Ute Mountain Ute, Hopi, Navajo, Zuni, and Uintah and Ouray Ute, have brought a proposal to Washington, D.C., to ask President Obama to protect 1.9 million acres around Bears Ears as a national monument. These 1.9 million acres are all public lands, held by the United States government—but right now, they are unprotected.

This first-of-its-kind national monument proposal is a strong statement that we, as Native Americans, are a part of the solution. We are the circle that surrounds the box, where the policies and laws live. We are here to provide education, support, and

" Join us in encouraging the spirit of healing. "

solutions, and we are also asking for our seat at the table, to help collaboratively manage the lands of our ancestors once a national monument is created. The Antiquities Act was passed to protect antiquities, but it should also honor the connections Native Americans still have to the land by giving us a voice in decisions about how our ancestral lands are managed.

Native Americans have always maintained a relationship with the land. Bears Ears is home to the dwellings of our ancestors, the final resting places of our people, and sacred areas where our people still collect traditional herbs and medicines today. But it is also home to oil and gas and potash. Like so many ancestral lands, the Bears Ears is threatened not only by looters and grave-robbers, but by mining and oil and gas companies, all of whom are inflicting wounds.

The land and its precious resources need to be healed, but there are other wounds as well, which is why healing forms the inner core of our Bears Ears movement. Relationships between tribal nations have been healed as we work together toward a common goal. And now the Bears Ears Inter-Tribal Coalition is looking to heal the relationship with the United States government. We are not wielding the hatchet of war, but rather extending our hand to say: join us in encouraging the spirit of healing.

We understand the work is vast, and disagreements are sure to come, but we are all seated at the same table, actively engaged, ready to learn from one another, encouraged by our elders, ancestors, and the many tribes who support our efforts.

Once a national monument is created, we must work together to help educate visitors, locals, and, most importantly, the younger generations. We must listen to the history of the early settlers and their stories and historical connections to this area to make sure existing and future management plans are founded on a clear understanding of the value of this land.

We believe Bears Ears should be protected, for all people. The laws exist to make this a reality. It is up to Native Americans to ask the United States government to use these laws to protect these lands, which are part of our past and our present. We are all human beings, breathing in the same air, walking on the same land. We are all citizens of the same United States of America.

REGINA LOPEZ-WHITESKUNK
b. 1969

We are the circle

that surrounds the box,

where the policies and laws live.

compromise/

a coming to terms or an agreement by mutual concession

compromised/

exposed to risk, danger or discredit; damaged

ON COMPROMISED GROUND

 don't hail from Utah, though I once lived in the neighboring state to the east. Nor do I belong to tribal groups for whom this is ancestral homeland. Still, I know southern Utah's rock-lands as a pilgrim, a writer, an earth scientist, and as a woman whose skin color resembles this earth.

And I've returned over decades, since that first childhood visit to Zion, Bryce, and the Grand Canyon with my parents. I've roamed from St. George to Vernal, Cisco to the Four Corners. I've geologized in the Henry Mountains. Taken the Burr Trail and the road over Boulder Mountain when both were unpaved. Dined at La Buena Vida Cantina in Caineville, surrounded by petrified wood. And I've hiked these lands: San Rafael Swell, Waterpocket Fold, Grand Staircase, Escalante canyons, Cedar Mesa, Bears Ears, Dark Canyon, more.

Aridity conspires with erosion to expose Earth's anatomy in the plateau and canyon country. Dry land and light draw me.

A century and a half ago, geological reconnaissances sketched plausible models for land-shaping forces here. It was in these drylands that geology came of age as a science in America, as field ideas became theories explaining uplift and erosion, intrusion

**" Aridity
conspires
with erosion
to expose
Earth's
anatomy in
the plateau
and canyon
country.
Dry land
and light
draw
me.**

and volcanism. It was in these lands, too, that beholding eyes from the humid East, eyes that once might have spurned canyons and deserts as barren and worthless, began to see in new ways—seeding perspectives that tourists now bring on every visit.

Yet by viewing Utah's public lands as isolated, unconnected pieces, whether wilderness areas or BLM oil-and-gas leases, one can easily miss the *whole* of the landscape, its ecological and geological integrity. Taken together the public lands of the plateau country—from the Grand Canyon to Dinosaur—offer not only unparalleled windows into Earth's deep history but also fragile, dynamic ecosystems that remain largely intact.

The Utah Public Lands Initiative now threatens this integrity.

Although touted as a "grand bargain," the proposed legislation fails at being a true compromise that balances development with conservation and outdoor recreation. The quality and health of these landscapes would be compromised, instead, by its passage. That this bill comes in the centennial year of the National Park Service makes the lack of mutual concession all the more glaring.

If the PLI becomes law, the Department of the Interior would lose some of its power to protect existing units or add further holdings. New "National Conservation Areas" might be conserved in name only. Oil and gas yields could be offset by longer-term impacts:

fragmented and degraded habitats, polluted water, diminished air quality within viewsheds of iconic parklands. And years of collaborative decision-making between agencies, communities, and other "stakeholders" over land use, which was pioneered by the Master Leasing Plan process, would become null and void.

Southern Utah's public lands can thrive for all of the people. And landscape-scale planning at its best must recognize interconnections, balance, and the significance of historical, cultural and natural elements.

These are goals of the Bears Ears Inter-Tribal Coalition, a remarkable partnership of the Hopi, Navajo, Uintah and Ouray Ute, Ute Mountain Ute, and Zuni nations supported by many more tribal groups. These peoples long invested themselves in their homelands, incorporating the land into their defining experiences. Ancient sites, artifacts, petroglyphs and pictographs are memory traces of ancestral pasts that are part of the land itself. The coalition has asked the president to designate the region between Canyonlands and the Navajo Nation as Bears Ears National Monument.

Yet the disrespect shown to coalition leaders, particularly women, and their proposal by some Utah lawmakers and residents reminds me of the writings of Zitkala-Sa (Lakota-Dakota) and Sarah Winnemucca (Paiute). More than a century ago both women noted close links between Euro-American racist attitudes of privilege and environmental attitudes that led to degradation of what had been Indigenous land.

If the issue comes down to dollars and cents for lawmakers, then they might consider this: In 2015, visitors to National Park Service lands in Utah spent more than $844 million in local gateway communities. The NPS documents that these expenditures supported 14,400 jobs, and generated nearly $436 million in labor income and more than $706 million in value-added. Park visitors contributed $1.3 billion to Utah's economy last year.

I've often wondered if it's possible to refrain from dis-integrated thinking and a fragmented understanding of human experience in this country. I've wondered if it's possible to refuse what alienates and separates. Any true coming to terms or honest agreement by mutual concession requires that we do more. It requires respect, the willingness to look again and again, assumptions put aside. Otherwise, without true compromise, we will be left standing on compromised ground.

LAURET SAVOY

STONE THAT LEAPS
A Utah Sequence

Preternatural strands,
the gesture of reaching.
Held as earth, just so.

—

The raven's gurgle
is a cat with wings, purring
quick to canyon echo.

—

Cold, full moonrise framed
by Partition Arch. Portals
to fins, mesas, dusk-

—

Bushtits. Then thumper
trucks? Thus an arch: silent.
Erosion's revenge.

—

I am 43.
Birthday moon, cold wine, firelight.
Stupid smile! Years of this!

—

Ravens tumbled as
I set up the tent, missing
you, the moon a blue juniper berry.

–

Mormon tea,
like crinoid columns
of a former sea.

–

And sandstone's slow cascade:
This place.
Lifted, cracked and stilled.

–

Wind-drift sand, sunlit:
How to make eons,
stone that leaps.

–

To thought's last thought:
Balanced Rock:
Wisdom's cairn.

CHRISTOPHER COKINOS
b. 1963

Whatever is left of solace,
of silence, of astonishment
and spiritual renewal, that is what
will sustain our children.

WHAT SHALL WE GIVE THE CHILDREN?

n the sandy bank of the San Juan River, I stood beside a small girl and her grandmother. "Have you heard of the proposal to protect all this land, from here to the Canyonlands?" I asked the woman. "What do you think?" She put her arm around the child's shoulders and studied the sun-streaked cliff.

"We have to save everything we can," she said quietly. "We have to save it for the children."

Yes, I thought but did not say. Whatever is left of the world when the extractive industries get done with it, that's the world our children will live in. Whatever ferocious winds and droughts are unleashed by climate change, those are the forces they will have to endure. Whatever plants and animals survive the accelerating extinctions, these species will be the only branches left on the storm-torn evolutionary tree of life.

It's true also that whatever is left of the world's diversity of cultures, the languages and lifeways, the songs and stories under global siege—those are the high peaks from which the human imagination will take flight. And whatever is left of solace, of silence, of astonishment and spiritual renewal, that is what will sustain our children after we have done our work, for good or ill, and disappeared.

What will be our legacy for those who have no voice to shape their own destinies—what chance of gladness, what landscapes of enduring, bedrock value?

When people talk about the values of wildlands, they justly cite the importance of economic storehouses, ecological seedbanks, and deeply meaningful cultural legacies. As I sit here in the whispers of yellow warblers and sliding water, the values that speak most strongly to me are the *spiritual* values—all that would be lost to the imagining and feeling part of the human mind, if these lands were penetrated by pumpjacks and torn by tires.

Let us give the children the flow of time. Here in bedded canyons, a person comes face-to-face with the deep history of the planet and the continuity of unfolding life. There is comfort in this, a bodily awareness of the immortality of substance and the constancy of change, the link to past and future, the assurance that we all came from the Earth and, when the time comes, we will be folded back into its arms.

Let us give the children immensity. In a landscape of this expanse and grandeur—1.9 million acres of redrock canyons, piñon-juniper forests, mesas, and rivers—our children will come into intimate contact with a reality far greater than themselves. The canyons are graced by beauty they did not create, carved to depths they can scarcely fathom, and shaped by forces they cannot control. A landscape of this size invites humility and awe. Who are we humans, we small creatures in the shadows of great walls?

Let us give the children wonderment, radical amazement at the mysteries of the desert on this majestic scale and in this microscopic exactitude, the expanse of the stars, the polliwogs in plunge pools. These are wonderful beyond imagining. In a secular world, stripped of all but material meaning, weary with worry, this encounter with the marvelous will be a blessing of great value.

Let us give the children tranquility. From my perch on the sand-bank, I can hear the flick of the stream across stones. Now and then a birdsong tumbles down the canyon wall. But the canyon hushes all the voices of the mundane, mechanical world. Silence collects under the deep-cut banks. In the winds, the coyote willows sing of the peace of a place that is protected from plunder. Here, in the soaring architecture of draped stone and silence, our children will enter into a place of gratitude and praise.

Let us give the children a landscape that will not be despoiled, an expanse of land that will never be defiled, bulldozed or burned, never taken as spoils in a war against the world or sold off in a giant going-out-of-business sale. Here, our children can follow paths worn by the footfalls of people who have walked the dusty cliffs for millennia and have chosen not to destroy them. The landscape will be proof of the possibility of human restraint. The astonishing integrity of the land lifts our spirits and floods us with relief—a joy beyond thought, a direct awareness of worth, unmediated gladness.

Turning away from the cliff, the grandmother lifted a strand of the child's hair, blown free by the upriver wind, and tucked it behind her ear. I thought I would see tears in her eyes when she turned to me, for the sorrows of the small ones. What I saw instead was ferocious love, the clear-eyed determination to defend a world that nourishes the hearts of children.

Kathleen D Moore

KATHLEEN DEAN MOORE

MEMORY

Canyon wren notes descend. In my heart, a crescendo: of joy, requited longing, a sense of homecoming. Here, in this aridity, amidst scent of sage and cliffrose, I know who I am. I know my strength and how to carry its subtle, remarkable weight. Here, surrounded by barebones earth, my being is laid bare. My being is resilient and true.

Canyon wren notes descend. Geese burst forth from the banks, distracting us from nests, eggs, goslings. Cliff swallows swoop out of mud-daubed abodes, seeking sustenance. Sadly, it is too early in the season for nighthawks. I introduced my husband to nighthawks on a long ago desert evening.

"My love for you is a nighthawk booming in my chest," he told me. My heart boomed back.

Though our home is now elsewhere, the desert continues to hold our love story. It always will, long after it is otherwise forgotten.

Canyon wren notes descend. Reflexively, my heart swells. It encompasses this canyon, the vast desert, and all of the stories I have sown and grown here.

I am a visitor. And I am home.

Everything has changed.

I am now a visitor.

Yet I am also home.

"Mama! Mama!" she calls, needing me as much as I have needed this landscape. Can I provide her all that these stony expanses have provided me?

She is just over one year old. My name is new to her lips. The desert sun and sand are new to her skin. This canyon realm is new to her nascent awareness.

I have become a mother since leaving my desert home. Everything has changed. Doubt—regarding identity, aptitude, my very place in the world—seeps into the cracks of my painstakingly stone-built strength. My once sure steps falter. Alone, I was enough. Now, I am her all. Am I still enough?

Everything has changed.

The canyon, however, remains. Small beings above still swoop and trill. Small beings below still skitter, slither, and dart. Minor stream riffles still echo off towering walls, as loud as raging floods. The rising sun still tenderly touches sage and grasses, gentle in its brand-new-day affections. Life here exists in a state of certitude.

Amidst this seeming constancy, I remember: the stories I wove, the self I built, the successional loss and longing and love that grew from parched earth. I want to give it all to my daughter, neatly wrapped in balsamroot leaves, tied with horsetail ribbons. I want her to know what I have known here. I want her to know that she is the product of desert and the memories residing there. I want her to be able to return to a landscape—and a story—that endures.

"Mama!"

The utterance is urgent, but she speaks with a smile, enjoying the sensation of power on her tongue. She already knows my reflexive response to her voice, this word. I scoop her into my arms, delighting at the feel of her sun-warmed skin, the perfume scent as her small hand thrusts a flowered branch toward my nose. She wrinkles her face in mimicry of sniffing. "–Frose," she says. Cliffrose. A new word. The story continues.

Everything has changed. I am now a visitor. Yet I am also home. I am coming home to myself in a place that remembered for me.

"She's going to cry when she sees this," he tells his companion, gathering a bouquet of snaking, blooming cliffrose branches.

When he brings them to me, I bury my face in the fragrance, but I do not cry. I will save my tears for goodbye. For now, we are home in the blooming-place of our story. Now, it embraces us as three.

Everything has changed, but my need for the desert landscape endures. I need it as it is, as it has been, as it will be. I need that bedrock stability, a constant by which to measure the mutability of my being.

How else can I quantify the distances I have traveled? How else can I return home?

In a world where everything changes, it is essential to have places in which we can be touched by the untouched, moved by the immovable. It is essential to experience beauty and truth neither conceived nor altered by minds and hands. It is essential to have something beyond us worthy of our seeking and striving. Worthy of return.

In the desert's constancy is its wildness, and we are the caretakers of this rare and fragile longevity. In our hands, we hold the fate of the places holding our stories. Everything changes, but where wildness remains, we can come home.

Canyon wren notes descend. My daughter calls my name. Cliffrose blooms. A chest-bound nighthawk booms. This place is a container for the ever-evolving story. Without an enduring, stone-bound memory, who are we as individuals? Who are we as a people?

JEN JACKSON QUINTANO
b. 1980

A PLACE FOR MEDIATION

When a group of Native people lives several thousand years together on the same landscape, close to every living relative and their dead ones, and adjusts to changes of all sorts, ultimately an additive and distinctive indigenous knowledge will coalesce. Unfortunately, in modern-day land management practice, this kind of knowledge sustained and practiced by Native peoples has been dismissed as too esoteric or anecdotal. And recent conflations of conventional environmental science and indigenous knowledge speak to an optimism that has not been successfully realized. But this is a new era, a new occasion, and a different stewardship dialogue has finally emerged.

We are now witnessing efforts that will improve sedate and inadequate systems of cultural and natural resource management. Inclusion of Native peoples representing the source of local indigenous knowledge will be the keystone of a collaboratively managed Bears Ears National Monument.

We are aware that knowledges and management systems are transitory and fluid, and the old systems supporting only one way of knowing are themselves artifacts of humanity's missteps. Many old conventions in cultural and natural resource management have lost their purpose. If the protection of our

Inclusion of Native peoples
representing the source of local
indigenous knowledge will be the
keystone of a collaboratively
managed Bears Ears
National Monument.

nation's antiquities and lands is to become truly egalitarian and progressive, then there must be centrifugal answers to our problems. We will labor, co-labor, collaborate, and co-elaborate from the fixed center.

In the spirit of a just transition to genuine and virtuous collaboration, a Bears Ears National Monument will enable tribal and federal authorities to reach out and enlighten on equal terms: to decentralize power and leadership and share problem solving. Rather than oppose each other, there will be opportunities to allow multiple knowledges to speak. Let us bury the fit-in-a-box orthodoxy of one structured and established system of lands management. The current system is not even binary. It is not two systems; with one recognizing the other, it is one system. By virtue of collaboration we will pay tribute to voices of the land and its antiquity, as it should be perceived and understood.

One-third of the 130,000-square-mile Colorado Plateau lies within the sovereign nations of several tribes, and so if this nation proves itself to be truly egalitarian, we cannot base our efforts to protect our antiquities and natural resources in a single knowledge system. A Bears Ears National Monument will serve as a unique learning place where science and tribal traditional knowledge will work to manage Bears Ears equally, a place to evolve an informed and competent citizenry, a sanctuary for cultural, social, and intellectual mediation.

Bears Ears should not be declared a national monument because it is an ethical thing to do. It should become so because it makes sense.

I emerged to this world from my mother.
She is where all that I love began.

JIM ENOTE
b. 1957

SHASH JAA' FOLLOWS WHEREVER I GO

BROOKLYN, N.Y.

early ten years ago, I remember sitting with friends in the back seat of a red Jeep en route to Salt Lake City and noticing the mysterious twin buttes jetting above the western horizon. I would later learn they were called *Shash Jaa'* in Navajo, or the Bears Ears. While driving through Navajo land near Mexican Hat, Utah, I saw these buttes tower above Cedar Mesa and connect to the Abajo Mountains, the lay of the land changing from red and orange cliffs to green forestry.

On this road trip, I learned that Shash Jaa' is where Navajo headman Manuelito was born in 1818 and where his ancestral Bit'ahnii clan call home. My political junkie acquaintances knew this, better equipped at Navajo history than this then-21-year-old. Their claims were later verified by Navajo historian Jennifer Nez-Denetdale, a descendent of Manuelito, and oral histories of Navajo families and clans, along with the testimonies from other tribes, nations and pueblos that have cultural attachments to this beautiful land.

Even though I was not driving toward Shash Jaa' during that

summer day, I was mesmerized by the Navajo connection. Instead of being attracted to the city life of Salt Lake City and the Mormon experience of Brigham Young University, my mind wondered about what the mountainous knolls, canyons, forests, water, and wildlife of the Manti-La Sal National Forest and surrounding public lands looked and felt like. I could only envision inhaling the fresh air.

Then last summer came. I was hired by the Grand Canyon Trust and Utah Diné Bikéyah to tell the story about the efforts of the Bears Ears Inter-Tribal Coalition, which I learned about from being a reporter with the *Navajo Times*. While at the base of the Bears Ears buttes last July, I listened to and talked with cultural leaders from the Navajo, Hopi, Ute Mountain Ute and Zuni people, who told how they continue to harvest medicine, pick herbs and minerals, hunt, perform ceremonies and issue offerings at designated places in the Bears Ears region.

Bears Ears will always be a significant healing space for young Navajos like me, who live in the concrete jungle that is New York City. "

Witnessing wildlife, including deer, come toward our campsite and listening to the Bear Dance songs by Ute Mountain Ute healers showed the connection between cultural leaders and Native families that want Bears Ears protected. Evidence of an indigenous footprint is obvious; more than 100,000 archaeological sites that date over 12,000 years reveal this history.

Unfortunately, these cultural artifacts are being desecrated, looted, and disrespected by non-Natives who see these sacred items as cash profits. Ongoing threats come from natural resource exploitation of the oil and gas and uranium industries and the environmental degradation of overgrazing by ranchers and all-terrain vehicles. This cultural landscape needs protection.

When I had my epiphany in that red Jeep, I never thought I would visit the Bears Ears in so many ways—documenting the July celebration of the coalition, camping, flying in a small aircraft, and learning the healing powers of this nearly untouched landscape, Hozho, or *there is beauty*, in the Navajo tongue.

I also never thought I would be writing about Bears Ears thousands of miles away in my Brooklyn apartment, where I attend graduate school at New York University. The presence of the Bears Ears Inter-Tribal Coalition is growing in New York City. At NYU, Angelo Baca, a Navajo doctoral student in film and anthropology, has screened his 21-minute documentary about the coalition's efforts and his family's connection to Bears Ears.

Bears Ears will always be a significant healing space for young Navajos like me, who live in the concrete jungle that is New York City. The experience of Bears Ears will always be in my heart and mind, just as it probably is for Manuelito, the Navajo leader who encouraged Navajos like me to get an education and help our people.

ALASTAIR LEE BITSOI
b. 1985

THE WILDNESS IN NATURE BINDS US TO THE PAST AND THE FUTURE

ince 1975, I have traveled to almost every corner of the State of Utah both as a citizen and as the former Utah BLM State Director. Every place I have gone inspires all of my senses. When you first see places like the San Rafael Swell with its buttes and knobs, canyons and washes, it all looks barren. But these lands are home to desert bighorn sheep, mule deer, mountain lion, coyote, golden eagle, waterfowl, and peregrine falcon, along with several rare plant species.

From the edge of the Wedge Overlook, I have stood in awe of the power of the San Rafael River to carve the deep canyon affectionately known as Little Grand Canyon. Many times I have returned to sit on the edge of the canyon rim to reconnect my soul to nature. You can feel, hear, and see the wildness of the area when you hear and see a hawk gliding on the rising air currents from the canyon floor. You can hear the roll of thunder and smell the approaching summer rain cells that cool the air as they move across the Swell. History and heritage come alive when you stand on the Old Spanish Trail nearby and close your eyes to imagine the trading caravans coming from Santa Fe, going to Los Angeles, and all those who walked this trail long before Utah was a state.

It is important that young Latinos come and partake of this wild country not only to connect with their heritage but to commune with nature.

This is a place I come to reconnect with my Hispanic heritage that somehow seems to be a small footnote in our history books. The names of places and the trails that cross this landscape remind me that others like me gazed upon the San Rafael country. It is important that young Latinos come and partake of this wild country not only to connect with their heritage but to commune with nature.

Public lands like the Wedge Overlook, the San Rafael Swell, or the proposed Bears Ears National Monument are places that hold our culture and heritage, where we can heal our hearts and souls, and reconnect with the essence of our humanity. Our grandchildren's children call upon us today to hold in trust these natural treasures for them.

JUAN PALMA
b. 1955

THE VIEW FROM THE MESA

From where I sit, I look into the sanctuary of my childhood. In my earliest recollections, my environment was just as far as my eyes could see. My world was the circular line of the horizon. This was the place that harbored the ancient gods and animal beings that are so alive in our legends.... The land is scarred with erosions of rain, yet the corn stands tall, offering yellow pollen for another year.

SHONTO BEGAY
b. 1954

THE UR-BEAR

voking the Icelandic concept of *land nam*, or the claiming of a landscape, the poet Gary Snyder tells us that naming a place is a way to absorb, participate, and be in it. So, Bears Ears.

These geological formations look like the super-acute hearing apparatus of a very big bear indeed and give this place its name. The bear in question is submerged in the landscape, rising from or sinking into it. The bear and the Earth are not separate but mutually constructed. Both the naming of this place and the philosophy it represents come from the indigenous people who have lived here for millennia.

Black bears still roam Utah. Historically, grizzlies did as well. Indians continent-wide referred to bears, especially the grizzly, as "great-grandfather." Europeans share this association of procreation, respect, and wisdom with bear as well. The Teutonic word *ber* led eventually to "bear," and also to *pare* and *pero*, or "parent" and "father," which in turn are related to *generare* and *procreare*. Ber is also cognate with *fer* and *ver*... "iron" as well as "feral." The taxonomic name for the black bear is *Ursus americanus* and for the grizzly, *Ursus arctos horribilis*. The Greek *arktos* is cognate for "chief," with scores of related words like "archaic," "archbishop," and "archaeology" all referring to context and authority.

For most of us, bears have lost any association that includes an ursine role in procreating *Homo sapiens*. But science today makes the case that bears participate in balancing the geological, biological, hydrological and atmospheric carbon cycles. The environment they have helped create over millions of years facilitated the spread and success of humankind. Even as the Earth is assaulted by climate change, the relatively stable biotic equilibrium continues to make our planet habitable. The living world protects us, providing a buffer for withstanding extreme temperatures and weather events.

Bears move energy around. They dig for tubers and bulbs, aerating the soil and stimulating plant growth. In defecating at a different location from where they ate them, they disperse nutrients from berries and nuts. These effects are especially consequential because bears are big. They eat carbon in one form, sequester it in another, and release it back into the overall system. The raw power of photosynthesis is thus transformed into the substance of further life forms, eventually decomposing and helping to create soil.

Bears are gardeners who design the landscape by eating, pooping, and making long

The bear in question is submerged in the landscape rising from or sinking into it. The bear and the Earth are not separate but mutually constructed.

sojourns to stake new territory. Bear lineages go back to the Eocene, 56-33.9 million years ago—so they have been making this Earth for a long time. The idea that a gigantic bear is embedded in the geography is more than symbolic.

Landscape is not just a pretty scene to gaze at or hike through. It is a living, breathing, energy producing and consuming entity that literally gives us our life. At Bears Ears, tribal people continue ancestral practices that include interactions with the landscape others of us don't quite understand. We tend to consider the sacred relationship Native people have with the land ineffable, abstract, an emotional rather than a physical thing.

One of the important reasons to protect Bears Ears is to allow Native people to keep fulfilling their covenant with Creation on this landscape. Today's world largely measures causality and value in numbers. We look to put those numbers into equations, to discern patterns in aggregated data points. I wager that one day we will actually be able to quantify the love, respect, and responsibility many Native people have for the land. The sums will be large. They will indicate that the transcendent is a necessary ingredient in the recipe of life.

So—develop more extractive industries on this magical, only glancingly understood landscape? Let's ask Papa Bear. He says no.

Mary Ellen Hannibal

MARY ELLEN HANNIBAL

With dozens of scenic redrock canyons, alpine peaks, forested plateaus, and plentiful opportunities for solitude, Bears Ears is truly a place worth protecting for future generations. Yet looting, grave robbing, ignorant visitation, oil drilling, mining, and irresponsible motorized use threaten to erase American history and damage a truly remarkable cultural landscape forever.

THE BEARS EARS INTER-TRIBAL COALITION

BEAR'S EARS

ear Campbell was a big guy, with big hungers, big Vietnam War stories, big appreciation for the ladies and a big love for driving the dirt roads of southeastern Utah. We picked each other up one April night in a smoky Flagstaff blues joint. It was 1985. I'd moved to Flagstaff from the east coast in January, fueled by Ed Abbey's *The Monkey Wrench Gang* and the conviction that earth-guerrilla raids and a guy like George Hayduke were waiting for me. Bear put his big arms around me for a slow dance and whispered, "You can call me Hayduke." Ten minutes later we were on the street outside the bar, playing wallpaper and wall.

The fourth month into what we thought of as The Road Trip, Bear called. "Meet me in Mexican Hat Saturday," he said. "I need a little solo camping first, then we'll have a hot and heavy night and take off in the morning for the Abajos. I've got a surprise for you."

I had no idea what the Abajos were, but it was easy to imagine the surprise. "You've got a deal," I said.

He stretched out his big ears.

 Behind him, two huge sandstone

buttes rose like the ears of a

giant bear.

I drove my '83 Firebird down U.S. 163 straight toward the burnt gold cliffs behind the San Juan Inn and wondered what would happen if my brakes failed. Bear stood waving in the motel parking lot. I pulled up next to him. "I figured I was going to be a grease mark on those cliffs."

He grinned. "Used to be a yellow stain up there. A guy driving a uranium ore truck didn't make the turn. Come on, let's get settled in."

We parked my 'Bird and headed in for an evening of fry bread, mutton stew, and spectacular romantic calisthenics. Next morning we took off north in Bear's old camper. We stopped in a weather-beaten Bluff trading post for watery coffee and the best homemade Texas toast I'd ever eaten. Bear whispered, "That's Mormon coffee. And that old lady that made it—I'll tell you outside." We took our food to the truck and ate on the way to Moab. "That old lady," Bear said, "gospel truth, she hired a desperado to kill her husband."

"Yeah," I said, "I can understand that."

Bear and I hiked up to Delicate Arch that afternoon, camped overnight on the shore of the Colorado River, then breakfasted on leathery fried eggs in the former mining town of Moab. Bear grinned at me over his Mormon coffee. "You ready for the big surprise?" he said. He paid the bill, bought me a disposable camera in the old drugstore and we headed back south. Bear turned northwest out of Blanding and navigated a curving dirt road, up from juniper, piñon, sage and soft green cottonwoods into a pine and fir mountain forest. We didn't talk much. He was hammering beers and I was too stunned by the beauty around me.

We camped off the road that night. Bear heated up beans and franks. "How you doing, greenhorn?"

I spooned up the last of the beans. "Do we have to go back home?" I said.

He laughed. "Time for you to earn your keep. I'll show you how to wash the dishes, rig the tent and set up our coffee for the morning."

"And," I said, "what about the big surprise?"

"Like we boys used to say in Vietnam, keep it simple, sweetheart."

I woke up before Bear the next morning, got the coffee brewing, and walked out the two-track to the main road. The scent of sun-bathed pine reminded me of my folks taking my brother and me camping in the Adirondack Mountains back east. A mule deer darted away from the road. I walked slowly back to our camp. "See any bears?" Bear said. I bent to kiss him. "Just this one."

We were on the road in an hour. "You ready for the big surprise?" Bear said. The road began to curve steadily down. "Close your eyes," he said, "and don't open them till I tell you." He drove further, slowed and stopped. "Remember, no peeking. Roll your window down." I heard him get out of the truck and walk away.

"Hey, Mary!" His voice was faint. I opened my eyes. Bear stood next to a sign that said Bears Ears. He stretched out his big ears. Behind him, two huge sandstone buttes rose like the ears of a giant bear. "Take your pic," he hollered.

Bear was gone twenty years later, killed by metastasized mouth cancer that had its origins in long-range patrols through Agent Orange-drenched terrain in Vietnam. I remember the picture I took that day at the Bears Ears, and how I had pasted it into my notebook, then ripped it up the night I learned Bear had left me for one of my "close" friends. Yesterday I hunted through those notebooks to find what I'd written about our trip to the Bears Ears, but the pages too had been torn away in anger. I can still see Bear's grin. That much is left, as well as the regret that I destroyed the picture and my writing.

I will always carry the memories of a golden forest dawn, and the hard knowledge that too much is gone—people, sacred lands, mountainsides, and ancient ruins—and we must fight for what is left.

MARY SOJOURNER
b. 1940

The bereaved [Demeter] lighted her torch and from Aenta's rocks cast the shifting glare of the mighty flame...as she followed the traces of the dark ravisher and the great wheel-furrows in the dust...[the giant buried beneath Mount Aetna] himself re-echoes her wild wailings and illumines her path with bursting fire...

The Rape of Persephone,

Statius, Thebaid 12. 270 FF: Latin Epic Cist A.D.

SEEING RED

The storm rolled across the sky like a chariot ablaze, hitting our mesa as I trudged up our dirt road to the garbage cans. Like a swarm of locusts, red dust pelted the trash bag slung over my shoulder while the two new pups—border collie-blue heeler brothers—dove for cover between my legs. Instead they rolled away like tumbleweeds. I tried to shout to them, but my voice and eyes were sandblasted, my breath snuffed. It felt like the end of the world.

For hours, the storm raged. Buds were scoured from the trees while tender green shoots were battered back into the ground. When it was all said and done, every fertile beginning had been laid to an early demise.

Even after the winds died, dust lingered in the air like sepia. And when the people of the Four Corners—the heart of the American Southwest—could finally make out the prominent incisions in our skyline—the 14,000-foot peaks of southwestern Colorado's San Juan Mountains—even the old-timers were amazed to see their snow-laden peaks coated the color of rusted metal. Not just flecked or lightly tinted, but thoroughly painted. From where I stood, looking at the eastern horizon was like looking through a telescope at Mars.

Jayne Belnap, veteran scientist for the United States Geological Survey, predicted this. By 2050, she anticipates that the region's soil instability "will be equal to that of the Dust Bowl days." Much of what gets caught up in prevailing winds is loosened by increasingly aggressive activities on Utah public lands, once-pristine places now ravaged by off-road vehicle recreation, oil and gas development, and livestock grazing.

 In the American Southwest, we dwell in one end of the visible spectrum. Passions or furies, we see it all in shades of red.

The proof was in the rivers. Satellite imagery would show that the dust on the snowfields had been lifted from denuded portions of southern Utah, an area blessed with millions of acres of public land—which includes the sacred and stunning set of formations known as the Bears Ears, for which five Indian Nations now seek permanent protection.

After crossing my mesa in southwestern Colorado, the storm dumped most of its debris on the snowfields of the San Juan Mountains, where the Colorado River's major tributaries—the San Miguel, Gunnison, Dolores, and the San Juan—originate. The darkened snow then absorbed the sun's heat, accelerating the spring thaw of the snowpack beneath it. In mad, incomprehensible torrents, the water rushed by—on its way to merge with the Colorado, which runs just west of the Bears Ears and the ruggedly beautiful, culturally rich Cedar Mesa over which they preside. Downstream, reservoirs were drained to accommodate the inundation. And then the water was gone, just as quickly as it had come. Meaning there was less water for big desert cities downstream.

As the swollen, grit-filled rivers raged by, we stood on the banks and watched, wringing red-stained hands. We turned to one another and wondered just how, come summer, we would quench our many thirsts.

That was seven years ago. But the red snow has occurred every year since. The water lost in these premature, riotous runoffs would each supply Denver for two years. This is on top of additional water loss associated with climate change, another seven to twenty percent annually.

In the American Southwest, we dwell in one end of the visible spectrum. Passions or furies, we see it all in shades of red. In the heat of the moment, we fail to remember, even in the face of climate uncertainty, the region's aridity, and the delusions of our own nascent mythology of the West. We saturate the land with promises, we project onto place the slaking of limitless desires.

I was born to this landscape, and still the only claim I can make honestly is this: to be a daughter of the desert is to have been born to Demeter, the goddess of fertile, fruitful sustenance as well as barrenness and famine. She rages and withholds, at our forgetting.

Red granules fall like dry tears. Somewhere above the fallout, I can hear my mother's wails.

AMY IRVINE
b. 1966

THE GRACE OF WILDNESS

The moment we hoist packs, the rain begins. It is four days before fall equinox; this is no spring mist. A horizontal wind slaps wet against us, and the cold stings our faces. Other problems soon become apparent: crippling blisters, forgotten gear, lethargy. It's a long walk, much of it in loose sand. The group's mood is sullen as the sky. Concerned about water, I try to hurry the students along, circling back with words of encouragement and offerings of dried fruit. They tolerate me—that's all.

Then comes our first grace: at midday the clouds blow off, like the unfurling of a curtain. We have descended deep within the canyon of burnished Wingate sandstone. The students get their first look at the lovely juxtaposition of redrock and Utah blue sky. The air remains sweatshirt-cool, even though the sun is out. Several days of rain provide a damp chill to the air. Fast hikers get stiff muscles waiting for stragglers, while slow ones get aggravated when everyone heads out just as they finally limp up.

It's now we receive the second grace of the day.

I round a bend to see one of the students running back toward me: "Tom! You've got to come here, quick!" She signals me forward and points at the wet clay in the wash bottom. Lying there, shivering on the cold mud, is a robin-sized slate-gray bird with muscular black feet and a broad mouth. In all my years as a naturalist, I've never had an encounter like this—a bird on the ground, for the taking. Recalling handling techniques from banding birds two decades earlier, I carefully pick up the bird, nestle its back against my warm palm, and brace its head between my first two fingers. Its eyes glisten with vulnerability and attention, but it remains motionless in my hand.

Though I have studied birds for over twenty years, I am disoriented—who is this? The visceral connection between the bird's fluttering heartbeat and the nerve-tips in my fingers focuses me on this animal as an individual being, not a member of a species. This bird man or woman, stunned by the cold, stares back at me. I feel power returning to its long wings. I carefully curl back my fingers and level my hand. The gray bird sits still for a few seconds, then leaps from my hand and flaps it long wings—once, twice, three times.

The instant it's in flight I recognize it as one of my favorite canyon birds, a White-throated Swift. It circles higher and higher above us. Then, from a nearby cliff, a second swift surges toward the first; they circle together, becoming smaller and smaller, and disappear against the red cliff. The individual being has disappeared completely back into the anonymity of the species. We humans look into each other's eyes.

"What was it?"

"Why was it lying on the ground?"

"How did you know what to do?"

I answer as best I can. *It's a White-throated Swift. I don't have any idea how it ended up on the ground, but once there, it was stuck—swifts are among the most aerial of all birds; they can only take off by launching from a ledge. How did I know what to do? I just followed my instincts, remembering the proper way to hold a bird, and watching its eyes very, very closely.*

We sling our heavy packs back on and resume our gradual movement down the canyon, toward water. But our eyes keep scanning the cliffs for the catapulting flight of swifts. The sky trembles with a new possibility. My fingertips still carry the lingering heartbeat of fear, and the joy of re-found freedom.

We humans cannot leap into dazzling flight. But we can access this tingling sensation—call it freedom, call it wildness—each time we enter these astonishing stone canyons. We feel it in the vibrating shade below numberless cottonwoods, or within the glow of shimmering evening light on polished sandstone walls. We hear it in the sound of water plashing over a rock ledge, and in the sudden torrent of a Canyon Wren's rippling song. And yes, we see it in the swooping flight of a swift. The landscapes that protect these simple, profound splendors are

We humans cannot
leap into dazzling flight. But we can
" access this tingling sensation "
—call it freedom, call it wildness—
each time we enter these astonishing
stone canyons.

found nowhere else in the world—which is why travelers converge here from every corner of the globe.

Are we really so eager to trade these startling silences and unadulterated beauties—these rare places that harbor freedom—for the same dismal grind and clang, the same acrid smoke, the same standardized monotony of industry's footprint? Why would we trade the rare elation of real freedom for the mundane ordinariness of plundering the world?

THOMAS LOWE FLEISCHNER
b. 1954

And the Voice said, "Moses did not go
to an oil well derrick to receive the Law
and the Tablets, and Jesus did not go to
a fracking site to give The Sermon, and
Buddha most certainly did not sit under
a pump jack to experience the vision that
changed the world forever. Sacred Place
is required to receive Sacred Epiphany,
and without that epiphany, wisdom
cannot be achieved."

.

IMPROMPTU MEDITATIONAL ODE CONCERNING
THE SACRED RELATIONSHIP OF TIME AND PLACE
(and the act of finding the bullseye in the center of epiphany)
DURING MILES DAVIS' "AUTUMN LEAVES"

and by an autumn inspiration
Richard Wilbur, "In the Elegy Season"

1

when silence screams like a gashed river
through the space between note and next
the mind makes the first movement
from absence to creation
    Parmenides all the while listening
questioning whether the basis is need
or dramatic impulse and if difference
is even meaningful, one can, like flotsam, turn,
move into a quiet pool of contemplation
    and begin the shift:
whether the fiction of this event we call life might
be akin to a small but very deep pond or even lake
the product of a thousand quiet pools and pauses conjoining,
co-mingling, creating in this instance the memory
    of an autumn perception
seen perhaps once in magical childhood

as from a great and fearful height nestled
in the remembrance of Bears Ears, Hatch Point, or Boulder Mountain
surrounded by huge vistas, great pines
    interlaced with the blaze of glistering aspen
all mirrored in the still twilight water
of a brilliant afternoon lake,
a reflection of first moment
personal realization that if autumn comes
    winter is not very damned far behind

2

and then the requisite shift
to antistrophe, the fulcrum moment
between inspiration and expiration
when the lips purse and in the mind
    the millisecond of doubt
the lake, great mountains, burning aspen,
towering and reflective pines memory
only symbols inviolably intertwined
with their referents
    covering what lies below
dark, incomprehensible and invisible truth
whispering in the embrace of acrophobia:
surrender, make the leap into the still stare
of water under moon-bitten pines
    sink into the dark abyss of unknown
the plunge, penetration of time's scrim
the lung throb, turn back toward surface
the second terror of suffocation
clasping the mind in fingerstops of nightmare

3

    then the awakening with the break into light
only to recognize the separation between aye and I
and remain standing above the lake's great eye
wondering: what next? while deep in the mind's ear
between the anvil and stirrup of memory
    the benign inner voice of enlightenment,
first comprehension that the shock
of height or drowning is not of falling or suffocation,
but of failure to make the leap, and with grace,
so that when the plunge comes, the remembrance
    thou shalt not fall: dive
into expiration, then new inspiration
and with that parabolic breath the mind returns
to blood rush rhythm, joy of the leap with the float
back into melody, which, as they say, is exactly why
    the beat goes on and on

Put off the shoes from off thy feet,
for the place where thou standest
is Holy Ground
Exodus 3:5

DAVID LEE
b. 1944

Our beliefs might differ,
but our values harmonize
on this essential point: wilderness
teaches us humility, wonder,
respect, and gratitude for
the Creator.

FAITH AND THE LAND

y Mormon faith has some of the most earth-friendly doctrines of any religion in the Judeo-Christian tradition, teaching that plants and animals are "living souls" and that the Creation is intended to "please the eye and to gladden the heart... to strengthen the body and to enliven the soul... for unto this end were they made to be used, with judgment, not to excess, neither by extortion" (Doctrine and Covenants 59:18-21).

As a practicing Mormon, I can't understand how Utah's recent efforts to seize public lands are consistent with such judgment. The same politicians who push for state control of public lands emphatically deny that climate change is real and human-caused. They support expanding fossil fuel extraction and neglect alternative energy sources. They reject or delay legislation that we desperately need to improve Utah's poor air quality.

In 2010, I participated in Utah's Faith and the Land initiative. Dozens of citizens gathered in small communities of faith—Quakers, Episcopalians, Jews, Mormons, and others—to discuss the value of wilderness in our spiritual lives. A remarkable consensus emerged that articulated our need for these lands as sources of spiritual renewal. Representatives from each faith group went to the Utah State Capitol building to speak directly to our legislators. What I said six years ago bears repeating today.

"Our beliefs might differ, but our values harmonize on this essential point: wilderness teaches us humility, wonder, respect, and gratitude for the Creator. Wild beauty has a special quality: its joys are spiritually meaningful because they are unexpected, like grace. Wild beauty teaches us about our small but important place in a diverse, complex, and interdependent world and inspires the moral value of self-restraint.

We are on a clear path to privatize, develop, and ruin every last wild and beautiful place in America. As the great Mormon thinker Hugh Nibley once said, "The appreciation of beauty is nothing less than the key to survival." When we get to the point where beauty is dispensable, we are in trouble. Wild beauty is a gift that requires our best stewardship.

It is human arrogance, however, to assume that stewardship gives us unbridled license to do as we please to nature or to act in short-term interest only. It is wrong to assume that nature always needs human development and improvement in order to have value or that only fossil fuels are God-given but not wind or sun. As we read in the Bible, the world is "very good" all on its own. God commanded Adam and Eve to "dress" the garden but also to "keep" it and "take good care" of it. Of course, there is a place for gardening, extracting needed resources, and developing land. But if we assume we can use up nature without limitations or without having to use our judgment, we will not only ruin its remaining wild beauty, but we will degrade ourselves.

Deserts, mountains, and sacred groves are vital for our spiritual and physical health; they strengthen the bonds of family and community. To get serious about preserving wilderness is to get serious about living a more reverent and gentle life and honoring an indigenous past we have tragically ignored."

I don't pretend to be above ideologies of my own. I don't know anyone whose theology is pure. For this reason, religion should inspire self-questioning, not unquestioned self-confidence. The good judgment my religion calls for requires respect for the Creation, a spirit of service, commitment to listen to others, and concern for future generations. We are not owners. Land is not an instrument we should use or own to shore up power and identity over and against others. It is, instead, good in and of itself, and we are merely its stewards. While we use the land every day, when we do so with deeper deference and reverence, we are filled with greater humility and dependence and wonder. We confront the fact of our own creatureliness.

If those who demand increasing state rights and extracting local oil reserves are motivated by a desire to be less answerable to the nation, to its indigenous past, to the planet, or especially to the Creator, then I want nothing to do with their demands. *I call upon all our elected leaders to protect Utah's public and shared heritage of extraordinary wild lands.*

GEORGE HANDLEY
b. 1964

LEASE UTU91481

'd driven past this point of cliff, this long rim, this mythic landscape fifty times and marveled at that wild expanse. Huge smooth gray ridges are laced with giant boulders eroded from the castle and cliff above. The land here had just taken its first spring breaths.

The Rim Road runs east to west along the first prominent ledge as the Book Cliffs rise from the valley. This road marks the southern boundary of the Eastern Book Cliffs Unit Wilderness Proposal. Prairie dogs called out, warning each other of our presence. Dry stalks of last year's buckwheat vibrated in the breeze. Months of cold, dark nights had sucked all moisture from the soil, turning it soft and frothy. Shadows of small birds flirted at the far edge of my vision.

This was early March in the desert. The awe I felt overwhelmed the knowledge that beneath me lay hydrocarbon resources, the rights to which we'd just purchased.

In February 2016, when my wife, Terry Tempest Williams, and I arrived at a Salt Lake City convention center to be part of a peaceful demonstration at the BLM auction, leasing this land for oil and gas development was not part of our plan. But, when the opportunity miraculously presented itself, we had no choice but to take it.

Beyond anything, anger fueled my reasoning: why are these wild and spectacular public lands being leased for as little as two dollars per acre? And how might our refusal to extract fossil fuels from these public lands increase the possibility that those who follow us might avoid the diminished future that global warming will bring?

Had any of the people in charge or any of those bidding ever been to our part of the world and seen these places? Have they ever experienced "awe" in the presence of natural wonders? If they had, I'm convinced, they could not act with such disrespect. Had they spent even a few hours wandering among the short plants and tall rocks, beneath the infinite sky, as one species among many, they might not think of these places as wastelands with values limited to what can be extracted once they've been dug or drilled.

I've been thinking about "awe" lately, inspired by the work of Berkeley psychologist Dacher Keltner. His work suggests that while experiencing awe, our self shrinks, opening us to more vast and expansive potential. Our desire to contribute to the greater good grows.

Were the energy developers at the auction immune to awe? Or are they too busy and

> **Beyond anything, anger fueled my reasoning: why are these wild and spectacular public lands being leased for as little as two dollars per acre?**

Solitude cannot be
mapped.

self-important to experience it? This may be a simple matter of looking too long in the mirror and not the mountain.

When we purchased the leases, the map we used was two dimensional, showing only sections and townships and roads. This golden castle perched against the skyline above these flowing grey skirts did not exist on those maps. Neither did these cliffs or these boulders. None of the topography. Of course, the map showed none of the sounds or movement or sense of soil pushing against my feet. Nowhere to be found on that map was this heavy quality of solitude hovering near the ground where I am careful not to trip and fall into it. Solitude cannot be mapped.

Now, eight months after our purchase, we're standing near the southeast corner of "Lease UTU91481." The November silence flexes under the pressure of oncoming winter. The last birds and insects surprise us. Prairie dogs scurry to prepare their dens, except the two watching the badger lounging in the afternoon sun. We have just been "denied" our leases due to our refusal to "use diligence in developing" them. That the most diligent action ever to take place on earth might be to leave carbon in the ground is lost on BLM officials. I know that this land along with the hundreds of thousands of acres bought and sold and drilled and trenched across this great desert is leased based on the lie that the highest value of these, our public lands, is the price of the carbon lying beneath them. At the very least, those desiring to lease our wild public lands should be required to visit them, preferably on foot. These landscapes need to be looked in the eye.

BROOKE WILLIAMS
b. 1952

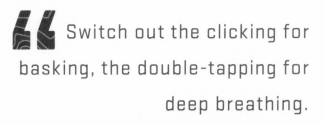 Switch out the clicking for basking, the double-tapping for deep breathing.

WE

♥

WILDERNESS

We were three and a half days into Labyrinth Canyon. If a canoe paddle had customized settings like an iPhone or a toaster, they would include: Meditative, Leisurely, Slight Corrective, and Pensive. For a while, ours were Frantic, Over-the-Top, Frenzied, or Sporadic. Only gradually we learned to tune in correctly—to red cliffs, blue sky, white clouds; colors rich and complex. Moments were infused with warm breeze and cool currents, bird calls and moonlight, rivulets of sandy sweat, the sharp stinging of bug bites.

Millennials, as my generation has come to be called, need what this wilderness brings: a wide open wonder and connection to land and people that cannot be captured by Instagram feeds or fueled by Facebook posts. This wonder nourishes us, becomes part of our selves. We are an exceptionally plugged-in bunch. Gazing down at screens, we click, comment, double tap, and swipe. We momentarily thrive on the pixelated gratification that comes with blue Facebook thumbs up and red Instagram hearts, convenient forms of connection, communication—even deceptive self-definition.

But switch out the clicking for basking, the double-tapping for deep breathing, the swiping for sweating under a sun framed by clear blue and reflected in river ripples, and even millennials slow it down, given a chance to absorb what is real.

On our first night on the river we set up tents and collapsed inside, before dinner and bed. On our last night, we stretched out on a beach and looked at the stars. Mysterious shapes appeared around us on the mudpacked sand: toads, illuminated by our headlamps, delicate-looking and spotted. As we drifted off to sleep, Kira sat up suddenly in the tent pitched next to mine. "I forgot my keys in Anne's car." This announcement was met with stunned silence. When we reached Mineral Bottom, her Jeep would be waiting for us but we'd have no way to drive it back to our starting point.

In the morning, a half-delighted shriek: Lauren had found a toad in our cutlery.

Later, having pulled our canoes ashore at the deserted Mineral Bottom, minutes after I'd waded back into the river for a dip—who knows how long we'd be waiting—a rickety shuttle pulled up, depositing a bachelor party onto the shore. I'm sure we gave the groom and his friends a promising start to their pre-wedding venture: four women in various states of undress and distress running toward them, clutching clothing, waving arms.

> "Even millennials slow it down, given a chance to absorb what is real."

We hitched a ride with the shuttle's driver, Doug, a grizzled, ruddy-skinned man who listens to Vivaldi every morning ("Gets my thoughts in line.") and longs for the good ol' days ("Used to be I wouldn't hafta call the shuttle company and charge you—we could stop by Ray's and shoot some pool and I'd buy you a beer"). We leaned back in our seats and watched time-layered cliffs go by, dry desert air playing through our hair. I closed my eyes, saw rippled sunshine.

Hearing about our trip, you might call it a disaster. But I'm left with the memory of vivid colors—of four young women in sunhats wading in water, walled by redrock and a boundless blue. I'm left with friendships strong with trust, my love for these friends rooted in toad-speckled sand and warmed by the sun, a trust shaped like *we will figure this out* and *where to next?* I've had many forays into wilderness since then, both with and without these friends. The awe does not diminish, it swells.

My generation needs public lands—as those before us did, and those after us will. Had we spent those days, not in the river-depths of a canyon, but lounging poolside, smartphones in hand, I might not remember that time in our lives at all, save for a handful of sunburned selfies that could have been snapped anywhere. We certainly would not be the same people, connected by a shared awe, a gazing upward.

ANNE TERASHIMA
b. 1989

IT IS THE LAND THAT TELLS THE STORY

Jacqueline Keeler

Once, when we were children, we stopped at Mesa Verde National Park, on a trip from Denver to visit my mother's family on the Navajo Nation. Climbing a ladder on a tour through the ruins, my sister tore off a fingernail. My parents comforted my distraught little sister and told her, yes, her nail would grow back.

We drove on until we reached my grandparents' house. There my grandfather, *ѕhi cheii*, and my grandmother, *ѕhi ma ѕaanii*, chided my mother in Navajo for taking us to the ruins. They fretted over my sister's lost fingernail, imagining darkly the spirits that haunted such places. The fingernail, in Navajo culture, is a personal item and often used in witchcraft. Its loss represented a foreboding attack on our family's happiness, our wholeness—what Navajos call *hózhó*, the harmony and balance with all things.

Our clan name is *Kinya'áanii*, Towering House, and some say we came from the ancient people who built those towering edifices, those ruins, seen throughout the *Dinetah*, our homeland between the four sacred mountains. It is also said (*Alk'idaa'jini'*) we were created by the goddess Changing Woman when she made the original four clans of the Navajo people. She rubbed her skin and fashioned my first *Kinya'áanii* ancestors from it. We were special because we came from her heart.

When I meet other Navajo people, the first thing they want to know is my clan. The first thing they know about me is my connection to Changing Woman, the land, and to the people. So often, as Native people we are marginalized and our existence excised in the stories told by the dominant society. So often we are never a part of those stories—whether they are in the Bible taking place in a distant time or place or when they take place here in America, today. For me to have a story that traces my origins, my identity, to the goddess' own body through my mother, to her mother and on back to that ancient time when we were first made gives me a place in the story of this land.

And it is the land that tells the story—stories go to the heart of who we are. When we live on the land these stories naturally emerge from the very environment and are told by our elders and passed on to the next generation and the next.

When my Navajo grandfather came to visit in my childhood suburban neighborhood, the other children were fascinated by him. He soon had a gang of followers on his daily walks. An old Indian cowboy, he looked like Crocodile Dundee. One morning, before he began his trek, he looked around for a good walking stick and found one in the yard next door. Our neighbor came out screaming in her bathrobe as he finished cutting down her new tree. But realizing she had met a real Indian (my grandfather did not speak English), she ended up thanking

him, grateful he existed at all.

You could still see cattle and even antelope grazing from our homes, but our streets were named for figures from Greek mythology. On Pegasus Drive, we and our neighbors planted the dirt yards of our new homes with emerald lawns and young trees, bushes, and ornamental flowers. But in our backyard, my mom grew a garden filled with towering corn plants, squash, and cucumbers that she pickled along with the dill she grew. Those smells filled our home in summer.

When my grandfather left our neighborhood to explore the ranchland beyond it, he stopped at the barbed wire fence that separated these two worlds. With his troop of children watching, he pulled out his wire cutters—he was a lifelong rancher, after all—and to our collective shock, cut the fence. That section of the fence was already bent, the wires pulled apart by joggers and our more adventurous neighbors, but my grandfather was different because he saw no separation between the worlds on either side of the fence. None at all. They were in his mind one and the same.

I was astonished. As a child I had no idea how these two worlds could be bridged. Watching him, I realized that they could be. His actions cut the veil that separated us.

I learned so much from my grandparents and they learned from living on the land, the *Dinétah*. It is the land, itself, that taught the Navajo people, we five-fingered beings, fallible and short-sighted as we are, traditional Diné cultural precepts like *hózhó*, living in harmony. And it is in places like Bears Ears, filled with ancient sites and habitats, where that learning can continue to take place. These places still have so much to teach us.

JACQUELINE KEELER
b. 1969

My grandfather was different

because he saw no separation between

the worlds on either side of the fence.

None at all. They were in his mind

one and the same.

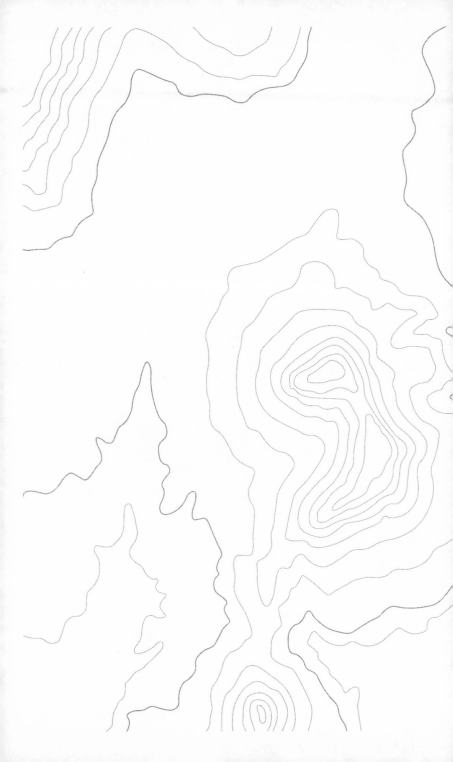

WHAT THE TORTOISE TAUGHT ME

The job was, by almost any measure, ridiculous. Every morning, I got up before dawn, drove to the edge of town, and hiked, alone, into the Utah desert. When I reached my designated post–the approximate location of Male 35, or Female 48, or Female 12–I dropped my gear in the shadows, found a flat rock, and settled in to wait.

Sometimes, wait was all I did. But sometimes, as the sun rose and began to warm the ground, I would hear a muffled scraping and grinding, as if the downstairs neighbors were rearranging their furniture. If my luck and patience held, a tortoise would drag itself into the open and, with an air of ancient exasperation, begin its day.

If it ate jawfuls of yellow flowers, I took notes. If it drank from a puddle, I took notes. If it had sex (a rare and precarious activity), I took notes. When, after an hour or three, the rocks grew oven-hot, the tortoise would lumber back to its shady burrow and I would lumber back over the desert, both of us returning at dusk for another round.

I was twenty years old, with half a biology degree and precious few practical skills. I'd moved to southwestern Utah, where I knew nobody, to spend a season as a field assistant on a desert tortoise research project. I was a shy kid, and like generations of confused loners before me, I'd been drawn to the desert because it looked like a refuge from messy human concerns: quiet, peaceful, and simple.

I could not have been more wrong.

Desert tortoises were, and still are, protected as a threatened species, and the project I worked on in Utah helped determine how much and what kind of habitat they needed to survive. But some of my neighbors saw the tortoises themselves as a threat, and their protection a harbinger of burdensome new regulations. Gas stations sold empty tins labeled "Desert Tortoise in a Can." During the years I worked in Utah, anti-government radicals in the region bombed two land-management offices and a van parked outside a Forest Service employee's home, shattering the vehicle while his wife and children watched. The biologists I worked for avoided talking about their work in public, fearing loogies in their French fries—or worse.

 These are the local voices—often quieter, but more thoughtful, more numerous, and ultimately more representative—that need our attention.

I spent three seasons watching tortoises in Utah. It was in many ways a dreamy time, punctuated by sudden, astonishing encounters with rattlesnakes and falcons. But I was increasingly fascinated, if often horrified, by the depth of human feeling surrounding the landscapes I worked in. Love, hatred, fear: even in the austere back of beyond, there was no getting away from any of it, and after a while, I didn't want to.

So after a final few seasons as an itinerant field assistant, I hung up my boots and became a journalist. For most of the past twenty years, I've lived on the edge of the Colorado Plateau, and written about the rural West. I've come to love not only the outrageous beauty of places like Comb Ridge and Cedar Mesa and Beef Basin, but also the region's habit of confounding stereotypes.

While the bomb-throwers—both metaphorical and literal—invariably claim to speak for the locals, most of the locals I've met prefer to speak for themselves. They're old-timers and newcomers, Republicans and Democrats, conservatives and liberals. They're scientists, tribal members, ranchers, and telecommuters, often more than one of the above. Some criticize the federal government, and some work for it. Some do both. Many are earnestly engaged in the grand experiment of managing the public lands, and many if not most recognize that experiment for what it is: an effort to manage local uses for the long-term good—the good of humans both near and far, and the good of other species, too.

This past winter, some of the anti-government crusaders I encountered years ago in Utah resurfaced in southern Oregon, where they led the armed occupation of Malheur National Wildlife Refuge. Though the 41-day occupation grabbed national headlines, locals widely rejected both its tactics and demands. In its wake, the county's longstanding collaborative conservation effort—one that acknowledges both local uses and the broader, deeper value of places like Malheur—has moved forward.

These are the local voices—often quieter, but more thoughtful, more numerous, and ultimately more representative—that need our attention. In southwestern Utah, after years of controversy, these voices helped protect the patch of desert where I once crept after tortoises, and proudly advertise the collaboratively managed tortoise reserve as a tourist attraction. In the Bears Ears, these voices are speaking up not only for themselves, but also for the rest of us, and for the future of the land. It's time we listened.

Michelle Nijhuis

MICHELLE NIJHUIS
b. 1974

WHOLE AND HOLY

The honey, bone, and amber-toned canyons in my Utah backyard are a magnet for tourists, drawn by the beauty of light on stone. I live at the gateway to the Colorado Plateau's wild canyons, places like Capitol Reef, the Bears Ears, and Cedar Mesa. Tourism and recreation are the lifeblood of the local economy. Wilderness is an asset just as it is with no need to pockmark the land with drill rigs and sprawl.

At night we see an awesome lattice of pulsing light across an obsidian black sky. Most visitors who stand under that spectacular firmament tell us it is the first time they've seen the faint veil of the Milky Way and the experience is breathtaking. The canyons that fall away around us offer endless recreation but also rare encounters with solitude and silence. There are vistas too vast to fit into cameras.

But after forty years of living in one desert or another, I know first-hand that America's iconic desert landscapes, places like Canyonlands and Arches national parks, are the exceptions, not the rule. The rule is that we dig up, dump on, scrape, bomb, drill, pave, overgraze, and otherwise abuse our deserts, most of them public lands owned by all Americans. We act as if there is no upstream, no downstream, nothing whole or alive in the middle of our schemes and deals.

Thankfully, there are exceptions. America's public lands are a vital commons where humans and wild creatures can co-exist, where a landscape hammered by heat has a chance to be resilient, where ecosystem health has a place at the table and the usual abuses are restrained. Our public lands offer us the opportunity to experience the land that shaped the nation's character. More than that, my wilderness experiences taught me that human life is embedded in nature. The food that becomes us is a synthesis of sunlight, rain, and soil. Soil is leaf, limb, root, bone, carcass, carapace, and flower. We drink from a watershed. We breathe each other's air. We live on a fluid planet where whatever goes downwind or downstream eventually settles into blood and bone. I know what is at stake because wild land grounded me.

It has also humbled me. I have wandered across Cedar Mesa and seen the crumbling towers, pot shards, and holy kivas scattered through the canyons. I have climbed the Bears Ears above mesas laced with ruins that demonstrate the crushing power of a harsh climate. I know that the deep and unique history of indigenous people holds valuable lessons for us today as we try to live within the carrying capacity of a changing world. It is time to empower tribes in the homeland they hold sacred. It is time to listen.

The great novelist Wallace Stegner sorted the conflicting impulses

I believe we have sacrificed enough

to the extractive compulsion of

 yesterday's Manifest Destiny.

It is time to swing the balance and

protect natural treasures from the

incessant blade of development.

in his native land into two camps. Nesters stayed to learn what the land could sustain while "boomers" pillaged its treasures and moved on. They are still among us, trying to frack and drill their way to Easy Street across our public lands. All of us have the urge to consume and move, as well as the urge to nest, so our choices are rarely clear or final. Ecological citizenship is the struggle to choose wisely and to live with each other's choices. Today, that struggle is intensifying in the American West as heat-parched forests ignite, reservoirs dry up, and sparse mountain snow is ever more stained with blowing dust.

I believe we have sacrificed enough to the extractive compulsion of yesterday's Manifest Destiny. It is time to swing the balance and protect natural treasures from the incessant blade of development. It is time to honor America's ancient history and to listen to those who tell a story that can help us understand our relationship to the land and our obligations to future generations. It is time to assure that our children and grandchildren and their children will be able to come here and be grounded, healed, humbled, and awed by the dance of light on stone. They too can stand under the stars and understand their lives anew because the Bears Ears will still be whole and holy. If we act boldly to save what is left, I believe they will bless us for our wisdom and generosity.

Chip Ward

CHIP WARD
b. 1949

WHEN THE DESERT MORNING RISES

While it was still dark, Dad would drive away in his Wagoneer accompanied by familiar radio voices; Mom was nowhere to be found—which meant she was already headed for the mountain to make offerings and ask for blessings; and I apathetically finished my homework. Mornings of separation made paths for solitary evenings on the mountain with Walt Whitman tucked in my backpack. The poet would ramble, and I would listen—a chromatic symphony of words to fill the emptiness where familial love should have nested.

I discovered hiding places: a mountain of trees was an obvious fortress; Whitman's acrobatic adjectives drowned out my youthful rage; and food kept me company. More mountains, more words, and more nourishment became solace for my abandoned home. My strategy was to smother my inner emptiness with overindulgence. I was willing to risk an emotional flash flood.

I married young, and my loneliness followed me into the marriage. I was determined that the feelings of abandonment would not consume me. My old strategy remained: more mountains, more words, and more food for both of us. But the flash flood eventually came when my husband of ten years said he never

 **When
the
desert
sun rises,
I hold my
broken heart
gently and feel
it mend each
time the wind
carries the
scent of
sage.**

loved me. Divorce was coming. Nothing in the days and months that followed could stop the wall of emotional debris that was headed toward me.

Alone, I take my questions to the redrock canyons of the Colorado Plateau. What more could I have done? *Nothing.* What should I do now? *Nothing.* Can I plant my hopes here in your sands and your rocks? *Yes.*

The desert is harsh, but it is real and visible. My old hopes and dreams would become a suffocating woolen coat in this arid climate if I did not let them transform into breathable linen.

This desert plateau is notorious for its stability and resistance to deformation. Over millions of years, it continues to transform like a diatonic scale—eroding in a sequential and harmonious pattern without many chromatic variations. The uncluttered ground here forms the space between the notes that truly creates the music. Between the notes, in the vast and honest open land, canyons absorb the darkness and redrock cliffs receive the light.

I wait for the next note.

The divorce came, and the heat of it kept me up at night. Yet, somehow, I knew relief would come in just the right doses at just the right time. Flash floods would eventually concede to a rhythm of enough rain. Enough. No more, no less. The wreckage would settle, and I would have what I needed. No more, no less.

There are countless places on the Plateau where, when the desert sun rises, sandstone cliffs melt subtly into vision—unassuming but undeniable; silent but articulate. I never thought I'd want to be like such a landscape: dry, stark, subtle, vulnerable, harsh, plain, vast, and ancient. But, now, when the desert sun rises, I can't be anything else. The Plateau continues to show me that enough is very little indeed. The Plateau continues to show me that enough is all I want to have and I want to be.

When the desert sun rises, I remember my parched and bare condition, and I find relief in its complete honesty. When the desert sun rises, I hear birdsong liturgies, and I sit peacefully in between the notes. When the desert sun rises, I hold my broken heart gently and feel it mend each time the wind carries the scent of sage. When the desert sun rises, I see that we are vast and ancient. When the desert sun rises, it is enough. This is enough. This is the Plateau. This is the desert I become.

Ann Whittaker

ANN WHITTAKER
b. 1981

UP BETWEEN THE BEAR'S EARS

was never much of a good earth keeper when I was younger. Like St. Francis of Assisi, I partied and sang and flirted and muddled my way through most of my teens. But then, a few things disrupted my hedonistic pursuits: a year-and-a-half-long illness; dropping out of high school; volunteering at the headquarters for the first Earth Day in 1970, and taking my first backpacking trip into Utah's Canyonlands the same month as Earth Day.

I say that the backpacking trip at the ripe old age of seventeen not only changed but saved my life. Within a year of it, I had somehow gotten into Prescott College (still without a high school diploma) and had connived my way into a ten-day backpack up between the Bears Ears.

After four days together, I was left alone for my first "solo" for another four days not far from the bald head between the Bears Ears, which reach up well above 8,500 feet. I backpacked further northward, into the ponderosas where a small spring and plenty of firewood had probably attracted hunters for millennia.

I set up my tent and sat, zazen-style, for hours on end, just listening. I hardly moved during the daytime. A herd of dozens of mule deer came up and grazed within feet of me, apparently un-perturbed by my presence, lingering hours within a dozen or two yards where I sat breathing and listening. Ravens and vultures circled my head, wondering if I were soon to be dead. Wild turkeys strutted through, more hurried than the deer and the ravens.

But it was the smallest of things that touched my heart: the lit-tle white bell-like flowers of manzanita bushes, seeming to have their own LED source of light within them. A few humming-birds—probably Rufous—on their way up to Alaska after winter-ing in the trans-volcanic belt of central Mexico. And the droplets of vanilla-scented pine pitch, which I chewed on whenever I got a little hungry.

I brewed up some Mormon Tea. I made salads of new shoots, flow-er petals, and leaves of God-knows-what. Otherwise I fasted, not famished but nourished by what I absorbed from the earth itself.

I was quietly nurtured by this place in every way. It lay before me like a seamless garment that stunned my heart, for everything there seemed to perfectly fit its place.

Then suddenly, it was time to walk out, to meet the other backpackers at our predetermined site, the smallest and most remote gas station I had ever come upon.

I went into the "office"—barely bigger than a pantry—and sat down on a chair near the entranceway to wait for my friends. There was a table piled high with magazines like *Look* and *Life* and *National Geographic*. The first page I opened had a feature about St. Francis of Assisi, whom the Pope had decreed "the patron saint of ecology" in response to that first Earth Day. A pull-out quote spoke to me, straight from the mouth of St. Francis himself:

"All which you used to avoid will bring you great sweetness and exceeding joy."

Seeing—almost hearing—those words in that little station on the edge of the wilderness suddenly put my entire life on another track. I have never been the same since.

I now try to focus my collaborative conservation efforts toward "restoring our common home" by considering such work to be my sacred duty. I struggle to resolve environmental conflicts through the lens of being a professed brother of the Order of Ecumenical Franciscans, a participant in the Franciscan Action Network, and a recent graduate of the Living School of the Center for Action and Contemplation. While I also still work as a conservation biologist and restoration ecologist, I don't think secular, materialistic or technological solutions alone will get us where we want to be. If the earth is sacred, as so many cultural traditions remind us, we must treat it as such and behave accordingly with our earthly skills and our spiritual values.

Of course, the expression of these values and vocations did not tumble out of me all at once, but this flow began to spill over and replenish me while I climbed up between the Bears Ears.

How can anyone like me ever repay that place, that chrysalis, for triggering my metamorphosis—my spiritual metanoia—that still

"How
can anyone
like me ever repay that place,
that chrysalis, for triggering my
metamorphosis—my spiritual metanoia—
that still informs my life
a half century
later?"

informs my life a half century later?

Can we protect it? Can we sing psalms to it? Can we bring it offerings?

What we can't do is forget it. We can't dismiss its global importance, its spiritual significance, not just to me but to thousands of other prayerful people who have made pilgrimages through it.

We have partaken of its communion of saints, along with Saint Redrock, Saint Manzanita, Saint Ponderosa, Saint Rufous, Saint Raven and Saint Vulture. Such experiences can never be shed, for they now live like mitochondria in each of our cells.

We have been inoculated with wilderness, and no antibiotic is strong enough to kill that out of us.

Gary Paul Nabhan

Brother Coyote, OEF aka
GARY PAUL NABHAN
b. 1952

A GESTURE OF PEACE

Op-ed published July 15, 2016, in the *Salt Lake Tribune*

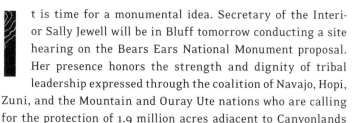 t is time for a monumental idea. Secretary of the Interior Sally Jewell will be in Bluff tomorrow conducting a site hearing on the Bears Ears National Monument proposal. Her presence honors the strength and dignity of tribal leadership expressed through the coalition of Navajo, Hopi, Zuni, and the Mountain and Ouray Ute nations who are calling for the protection of 1.9 million acres adjacent to Canyonlands National Park in the remote region of Cedar Mesa.

The coalition of five tribes—supported by more than 20 tribes within the American Southwest and the National Congress of American Indians, comprised of more than 250 tribes—is asking the United States government to see their home ground through the lenses of traditional knowledge gleaned through relationships cultivated over time.

I do not profess to know how Indian people feel. I only know how I feel when I am with them. I am drawn into a circle of relationships that widens my own sense of community that includes all living things. My debt is large to Indian people and all the ways they have shaped and influenced my own sense of home.

I believe the Bears Ears National Monument proposal honors the deep residency of native peoples living inside the Colorado Plateau. The tribes are asking each of us to acknowledge an embodied intelligence born of the land that warrants as much respect and protection as the wilderness, itself.

The Bears Ears National Monument proposal has the potential to transform Utah's rancorous politics of place into an ethic of place for generations to come.

Not long ago, 15 students gathered in our living room with Jonah Yellowman, a Navajo spiritual leader from Monument Valley. When Jonah arrived, coyotes began howling, a rarity at nine o'clock in the morning.

He entered our home, the students sat near him, and he began his remarks with a blessing. After the blessing, he spoke about how one learns, how his father taught him as a young boy to bring in wood and water at night, so that in the morning you will have dry wood to make a fire for warmth, and water to boil a cup of tea.

"You will not be caught short in a blizzard," he said.

He shared how he became a medicine person, how the ashes spoke to him, how if one holds a crystal up to the stars for guidance and then peers back into the ashes, one can see into the soul of the person in need. One of the students bluntly asked Jonah why he was sharing this sacred knowledge.

"It is time," Jonah said.

Jonah spoke about why these lands on Cedar Mesa remain sacred to the Navajo; how the bones of his ancestors are buried here, how their ancient songs are still carried by the winds, and how the Diné see these lands as their medicine cabinets. This is the

I do not profess to know how Indian people feel. I only know how I feel when I am with them.

"The tribes are opening the door, inviting us to cross a threshold where a more expansive conversation about land protection awaits us."

home of their ceremonies. This is the place where he remembers the source of his dreams.

"I have dreamed of being in this place before," Jonah said.

He pointed north toward the Colorado River. "The elders told me that this canyon where the great river flows was created by the bison from scraping the Earth with his hoof."

"It is time to go outside," he said. We followed him on to the patio in Castle Valley, where we witnessed a rare horizontal rainbow above the mesa.

It is time for us to go outside our own places of comfort and dare to embrace a new way of seeing. The tribes are opening the door, inviting us to cross a threshold where a more expansive conversation about land protection awaits us. They are taking us beyond the rhetoric of wilderness designation to a wider view of how we can live in place with reverence and restraint. Leaders like Jim Enote from the Zuni Pueblo remind us how these desert lands are "source, not resource."

In this centennial year of the National Park Service, it is hard to imagine a more profound act that could provide a greater healing between indigenous people and the federal government than this bold national monument. At a time when race has created a wedge and a wound within our communities in the United States of America that is anything but united, Bears Ears National Monument becomes a gesture of peace extended to disenfranchised people still held captive by the violence of our shadowed history.

The partisan politics that continues to plague public land policy in the 21st century is being offered a powerful corrective by collaborating with the tribes in a co-management model of cooperation where traditional knowledge is embedded within current land agency governing principles and practices. It will not be easy, but it will be transformative and right.

Our national parks and monuments are not simply "America's best idea" but an evolving idea. In their quiet and dignified manner, the tribes are leading the way forward with a vision of land protection in Utah that is at its core, spiritual. We are the sum of all our relations, both human and wild.

May Secretary Jewell listen to the collective wisdom of the tribes and carry it back to Washington and return to their native home ground with a monumental decision.

Terry Tempest Williams

TERRY TEMPEST WILLIAMS
b. 1955

IT'S TIME TO ACT

he Congress, led by the House of Representatives, has declared war on our land, water, and natural resources. And it is time for those of us who support our conservation tradition to raise our voices on behalf of the American people.

As these attacks escalate, the urgent question for those of us who support and advocate for our conservation tradition is how to respond. One alternative is to lie low, hoping that this storm will soon pass by without too much lasting damage.

Failure to respond, however, is a form of appeasement that has not worked in the past and it will not work this time. Our adversaries prefer to operate in the shadows, outside the sunshine generated by public knowledge and participation. For our opponents know that when anti-environmentalism becomes a public issue they will lose. They know that American support for our environmental heritage is wide and deep.

Out west, a coalition of Native American tribes has proposed a new type of national monument in southern Utah. Navajo, Hopi, Uintah and Ouray Ute, Ute Mountain Ute, and Zuni tribal members—the original occupants of this region—are seeking, in their words, "to work constructively and respectfully with the Federal agencies" to protect nearly two million acres of their ancestral lands.

Last October, the tribes submitted a petition to President Obama, requesting he use his authority under the Antiquities Act to designate a national monument to be called Bears Ears, after a distinctive landform rising above Cedar Mesa in the center of this region. Lands currently controlled mainly by the Bureau of Land Management, but also including some held by the Forest Service and the National Park Service, would be jointly administered by a partnership between the tribes and the federal agencies.

Tribal leaders are not demanding return of these ancestral lands. They acknowledge that public lands are part of our national patrimony, and should be held in perpetuity for the use and enjoyment of all Americans.

The tribes are, however, seeking a larger role in the protection of their sacred sites and access to places of ceremonial importance. Management of the land, they contend, should incorporate traditional knowledge and respect for the spiritual values inherent in the natural world. In the words of a Ute tribal member, Malcolm Lehi, "We can still hear the songs and prayers of our ancestors on every mesa and in every canyon."

The next move is Obama's. To be sure, he should request and consider responses and suggestions from all sides on the tribes' national monument proposal. He can shape or modify it on many points relating to boundaries, preparation of management plans, dispute resolution and the roles the Forest Service, the National Park Service, and the Bureau of Land Management will play.

The president has the power, the responsibility and the public support to stand up to those who would destroy our heritage. The Antiquities Act has, for more than a hundred years, granted the president authority to establish national monuments.

The best way to defend the Antiquities Act is for the president to use it.

These issues of enhanced land and cultural protection have festered long enough in Utah. The president should resolve them now by creating Bears Ears National Monument.

BRUCE BABBITT
b. 1938

> **"**
> The best way to defend the
> Antiquities Act is for the
> president to use it.

WALKING TO WATER

Election Day, November 2015

y wife, Maggie, and I paddled our pack raft from the historic gauging station on the east side of Lees Ferry to the boat ramp on the west. It was cloudy, cold, and windy, but we felt a quiet elation. We had just completed a 45-day, 400-mile walkabout from Upper Grand Gulch to Lees Ferry.

We'd started our initial walkabout in the early 1980s, traveling from Lees Ferry up the narrowing Paria, over the Kaiparowits Plateau down into the Escalante and circling the Henry Mountains. After 30 days and 300 miles, we stopped—temporarily—at Hite, at the top of Lake Powell. Three years later, we were back at Hite for a 300-mile traverse of the Dirty Devil and Maze Country, a swim across the Colorado River, and south to the natural bridges of White Canyon and cliff dwellings of Grand Gulch.

And now, 35 years, two children, and 16 years in Congress later, as we clambered out of our little raft at Lees Ferry, we'd completed our version of the Grand Circle in the most fascinating and mysterious landscape in the world.

I am a son of the Colorado Plateau. My father grew up on the Little Colorado and my mother in the high reaches of Rocky Mountain

National Park. John D. Lee, Mormon explorer, founder of Lees Ferry and, yes, of Mountain Meadows Massacre notoriety, was my paternal great-great-grandfather. Jacob Hamblin, the Mormon leatherstocking and trusted friend of the Colorado Plateau's Native American tribes, was my maternal great-great-grandfather.

From an early age, I was captivated by the natural, geologic, and human history of the Southwest. And, as we walked day-to-day in the wildest, most remote terrain in the Lower 48—some of which lies within the proposed Bears Ears National Monument—I keenly felt the presence of my own family's history, and of the people who, for thousands of years, lived in and on these vast, arid lands.

Below the Bears Ears buttes, I understood what this country can do for all of us. Here, we come as close as we ever can to sensing the power of the relationship that Native people have with their homeland. Here we reconnect with our own relationship to wild country. Here, as the Bears Ears Inter-Tribal Coalition so eloquently tells us, we have a rare chance for restoration and healing.

I kept asking myself what linked us to those humans who came here before us.

Awe and respect for Mother Nature and for the scale and diversity of landforms. Navajo Mountain, Monument Valley, Bears Ears. LeChee Rock, Nokai Canyon, Cummings Mesa. Intimacy and beauty in the turns of countless canyons, sculpture in every rock, the whisper of running water. The order and rhythm of life present in the flora and fauna, from the intricate patterns of microbiotic soil, to maidenhair ferns hanging on a shaded wall, to the elusive but always present coyote. That order and rhythm ultimately depends on an element miraculous and scarce, both in the universe and on the Colorado Plateau: water.

Every morning, as we packed up our gear, we faced the question: Where is our next water? How much water must we carry? Having ample water in your pack is comforting and—at least initially—liberating, but those feelings come at a cost. More than two quarts on your back perversely becomes oppressive.

You face a conundrum: water's weight slows you down and the more water you're hauling, the heavier your attitude becomes. But not having enough is also a burden. On a long, hot traverse of Navajo Mountain with only a half-quart each, our mouths dried up along with our mental fortitude. We hoped, and managed to convince ourselves, that there would be water in Horse Canyon. Alas, Horse Canyon was dry. A hot evening wind blew as we crawled under a juniper tree, husbanded our water and ate "wet" food (tuna, dried fruit, candy). We endured a restless night of unsettled dreams hoping the spring on the next day's map would be flowing.

A central challenge of our walkabout adventure was to learn to decipher the clues that lead to water.

Decades of desert travel have taught us some skills. Luck also plays a role. As it turned out, over half our nights we depended on potholes—pools of water found in natural rock cisterns of all shapes and sizes carved by wind and water over eons—where rainwater will sit for days, weeks, or even years. We were literally on our hands and knees praying to water, whether clear or

We were always

prepared to walk to water,

but what if the water

isn't there?

colored red, brown, or green. Its smell, feel, our gratitude, our desire, even our unspoken fear of dry camps were all part of our daily existence. So it has always been for humans who live on the Colorado Plateau.

In all of our southwest cultural traditions, there is a reverence for water. Every drop must be respected and cherished. When you must daily carry water, irrigate by hand, dig irrigation ditches, count on spring runoff and endure drought, you are mindful. Our technological prowess has allowed us to let that mindfulness slip. But science shows we have over-appropriated the waters of our river basins, and strategic campaigns are underway to reduce, conserve, and reuse our finite water.

Now a greater existential challenge looms. Climate change is not a theory; it is a reality.

It affects all we hold dear on the Colorado Plateau. Listen to Hopi and Navajo sheepherders, ranchers, water engineers, and river runners. Like the Ancestral Puebloans, they see it and feel it.

Here's the good news: we know what to do.

Carbon emissions must be significantly reduced, and soon. Historically, we have always taxed pollutants like mercury and acid rain. Carbon dioxide, by this definition, is a pollutant, and it is my long-held view that we should apply a fee to carbon emissions. American innovation will then meet the challenge and new clean technologies will emerge. The recent Paris Agreement is a huge step by the international community. Regionally, we in the Southwest can lead in deploying wind, solar, and biomass energy systems.

I will be presumptuous and suggest that Maggie's and my daily quest for water is a perfect metaphor for what our region faces.

We were always prepared to walk to water, but what if the water isn't there?

As I savor and relive our walkabout, I desperately want to know that someday, my grandchildren will be able to retrace our route. I want them to know the Colorado Plateau on foot. If they can walk to water as we did, I have to believe our generation will have met the challenge of climate change. The residents of our modern southwestern communities don't and can't walk to water.

The biggest pothole of all, Lake Powell, if not replenished, will only hold water for a few years.

But if water is present in the tanks and potholes, hidden springs and crevices, and during the summer and winter monsoons as it has historically been, and as it was for Maggie and me, we will have kept faith with future generations.

But it will not be enough to hope, as we did on the flank of Navajo Mountain, that the Horse Canyons of the Colorado Plateau will hold water. It is up to us to act now.

MARK UDALL
b. 1950

WE COME OUT DANCING TOGETHER

The leaders of the Bears Ears Inter-Tribal Coalition use the word "healing" whenever they define their relationship with this place. Eric Descheenie, coalition co-chair, says, "By protecting these sacred ancestral lands we can take an important step towards healing." Descheenie, a Navajo, emphasizes this "indigenous truth" as the foundation for all discussions about why the Bears Ears need our attention.

For Navajo leader Willie Grayeyes, "protecting Bears Ears is not just about healing for the land and Native people. It's for our adversaries to be healed, too. I truly believe we can all come out dancing together."

These Native people expand our boundaries for emotional bonding with the land. The writer Alice Walker takes us a step further. She falls in love with the characters in her novels. She understands their flaws and their struggles, and she's come to believe, "We can only heal if we see the wound."

The wounds in this land run both shallow and deep. But to respond to them, we must first see them. We can't see archaeological looting as barbarism unless we recognize digging in prehistoric graves as destruction. Unless we see the hundreds of thousands of cultural sites reaching more than 12,000 years into our past as the living heritage of today's Pueblo people. These artifacts, ruins, and rock art carry essential messages from ancestral elders to the Hopi and Zuni of our time and to all of us, reminders that failure looms unless we listen to this dynamic, fragile land.

For Native people, the canyons and mesas of southern Utah aren't "desert" or "wilderness" or "destination." These redrock labyrinths are home. For millennia, people have woven cultural identity into this ground. Wound the place and you wound the people. Take the person away from her land, and you damage her soul.

We can't understand Bears Ears unless we see the landscape for what it is, a living library of indigenous knowledge, a font of strength and healing.

———————

Our daughter says, "I learned two absolutes from my parents. From my mom, 'Always write a thank-you note.' From my dad, 'Don't step on the biological soil crust.'"

Wander through slickrock. Follow the cross-bedded, water-polished, mineral-stained sandstone between swales where soil collects, deepening a centimeter every thousand years. Castellated nubs of what looks like black crud shield this precious soil with a grid woven by microorganisms that stabilize and fertilize and prevent erosion.

Flatten that soil crust and you disrupt a fragile network of life. The first footprint or first bicycle tire track or first cow hoof does most of the damage. A thoughtless ATV driver doesn't see the

"We can't understand Bears Ears unless

we see the landscape for what it is,

a living library of indigenous knowledge, a

font of strength and healing. "

wound he leaves when he guns his four-wheeler off-road. He sees adventure. But he and his friends create a fretwork of tracks that fragments habitat. Burly tires tear the skin of the earth, and this dry land loses its stability.

After a one-time trample, pioneering cyanobacteria, the first and tiniest organisms to colonize soils, might take a decade to recolonize. Early successional lichens can take 60 years; the most colorful mature lichens often never recover. Climate-stressed soil crust will need centuries to regenerate.

Sever the invisible threads holding the land together, wound the soil crust at the scale of widespread overgrazing and energy development, and all that newly-released dust blows eastward into the Colorado Rockies. Red dust settles onto alpine snowfields. Instead of brilliantly reflective white snow, the darkened surface soaks up extra sun and holds the heat.

Snowmelt in southwest Colorado now comes 50 days earlier than it did when we set up our system for delivering water to 40 million people downstream. Our reservoirs can't store that overabundance of spring runoff, and so we lose water we'll need later in the season. The thirsty citizens of Los Angeles need healthy and protected soil crust at the far end of the Colorado River system, in the canyonlands of the Colorado Plateau, to secure their irreplaceable drinking water.

And so we must see potential wounds and avoid them. We must thread our way with care and restraint between patches of crusted soil. We must find the ribbon of sure-footing through the slickrock that leads to a secure future for the redrock canyonlands.

"I believe that only in diné bizaad,
the Navajo language, which is endless, can this place be described, or even indicated in its true character. "
—N. SCOTT MOMADAY

We must find the ribbon

of sure-footing through the slickrock

that leads to a secure future for the

redrock canyonlands.

Today, the National Park Service, the Forest Service, and the Bureau of Land Management administer the 1.9 million acres surrounding the Bears Ears buttes. These federal agencies often lack Native perspectives.

The coalition of 26 tribes and pueblos asking President Obama to declare a Bears Ears National Monument seeks co-management of these lands. As federal land managers grapple with reconnection, restoration, and protection in a Bears Ears National Monument, they will have allies in Native America. None of us, BLM scientist or Ute rancher or urban pilgrim, can hold up our end of our lifelong relationship with the redrock wildlands unless we remember to listen to all, to be tender and aware, to watch for unseen wounds. To never step on the soil crust.

And to remember to send thank-you notes. Since we are reminding ourselves of absolutes, I'll prepare my note of appreciation now, poised to hit "send" when the time comes to celebrate the president's vision.

Dear President Obama:

Thank you for designating America's richest unprotected cultural treasure as the Bears Ears National Monument, a place of learning, sanctuary, and healing.

Thank you for thinking big and protecting a large landscape capable of resilience in the face of change. Thank you for acting on behalf of our grandchildren, on behalf of the last canyon treefrogs singing in Slickhorn Gulch along the San Juan River. On behalf of the Navajo medicine man gathering herbs on the forested mesas of the Bears Ears.

Thank you for creating this never-before-dreamed-of moment of reconciliation.

In gratitude,

STEPHEN TRIMBLE
b. 1950

STAND UP FOR THE REDROCK

We have extended the reach of a conventional book by creating an interactive multimedia website, **www.redrockstories.org**, to gather good work in all media inspired by southern Utah's redrock wildlands. The pieces in *Red Rock Stories* form the bedrock for this nexus of responses to the Utah redrock wilderness. We invite you to contribute your own "testimony," your own creative responses to this land.

KEEP UTAH WILD WITH YOUR SUPPORT OF:

SOUTHERN UTAH WILDERNESS ALLIANCE / suwa.org

GRAND CANYON TRUST / grandcanyontrust.org

UTAH DINÉ BIKÉYAH / utahdinebikeyah.org

THE WILDERNESS SOCIETY / wilderness.org

THE NATURE CONSERVANCY / nature.org

SIERRA CLUB / sierraclub.org

WILD UTAH PROJECT / wildutahproject.org

TORREY HOUSE PRESS / torreyhouse.org

CONTRIBUTORS

BRUCE BABBITT served as Secretary of the Interior from 1993 to 2001, as governor of Arizona from 1978 to 1987, and as attorney general of Arizona from 1975 to 1978. He pioneered the use of habitat conservation plans under the Endangered Species Act and worked with President Bill Clinton to create or expand twenty-two new national monuments, beginning with Utah's Grand Staircase-Escalante National Monument.

SHONTO BEGAY (Navajo) spends his time painting and speaking to audiences of all ages. Begay was born in a hogan in Shonto, Arizona. His father is a medicine man, and his mother weaves rugs and herds sheep. He worked as a National Park Service ranger for ten years at Grand Teton National Park and Navajo National Monument. A professional artist since 1983, his work has been shown in more than fifty galleries and museums.

ALASTAIR LEE BITSOI (Navajo) is a freelance writer from Naschitti, New Mexico. He worked as a reporter for the *Navajo Times* from 2011 to 2015, and is pursuing a graduate degree in public health from New York University's College of Global Public Health.

CHRISTOPHER COKINOS is an associate professor of English at the University of Arizona and author of several books, including *The Fallen Sky: An Intimate History of Shooting Stars* and *The*

Underneath. Co-editor of *The Sonoran Desert: A Literary Field Guide*, he is the former head of the Utah Audubon Council and the Kansas Audubon Council. His awards include a National Science Foundation Antarctic Visiting Artist and Writer Fellowship and a Whiting Award. He divides his time between Barrio Libre in Tucson, Arizona and Logan Canyon, Utah.

JIM ENOTE, a Zuni tribal member, high altitude traditional farmer, and interrupted artist, is the director of the A:shiwi A:wan Museum and Heritage Center and director of the Colorado Plateau Foundation. He serves on the boards of the Grand Canyon Trust and Jessie Smith Noyes Foundation. Enote is a National Geographic Society Explorer and New Mexico Community Luminaria and received the Guardian of Culture and Lifeways Award from the Association of Tribal Archives, Libraries, and Museums.

THOMAS LOWE FLEISCHNER is the founding director of the Natural History Institute at Prescott College. He has conducted field studies from Alaska to Antarctica and co-founded the North Cascades Institute in Washington State. A naturalist and conservation biologist, he is the author of two books—*Singing Stone: A Natural History of the Escalante Canyons* and *Desert Wetlands*—and editor of *The Way of Natural History* and the forthcoming *Nature, Love, Medicine: Essays On Healing In Wildness.*

DAVID GESSNER has written ten books, including *All the Wild That Remains: Edward Abbey, Wallace Stegner and the American West* and *Ultimate Glory*, a memoir and history of Ultimate Frisbee. He has won the John Burroughs Award for Best Nature Essay, a Pushcart Prize, and recently hosted *Call of the Wild* on the National Geographic channel. Gessner taught Environmental Writing as a Briggs-Copeland Lecturer at Harvard and is now chair of the Creative Writing Department at the University of North Carolina at Wilmington.

GEORGE HANDLEY is professor of Interdisciplinary Humanities at Brigham Young University. He co-edited *Stewardship and the Environment: LDS Perspectives on Nature* and is the author of the environmental memoir, *Home Waters: A Year of Recompenses on the Provo River*. A founding board member of LDS Earth Stewardship, he has served as a trustee of the Utah chapter of The Nature Conservancy, member of the Sustainability and Natural Resources Committee for the city of Provo, and board chair of Utah Interfaith Power & Light.

MARY ELLEN HANNIBAL is an award-winning journalist and author. Her most recent book, *Citizen Scientist: Searching for Heroes and Hope in an Age of Extinction*, was named one of the best of 2016 by the San Francisco Chronicle. The book combines history, science, and memoir to both better grapple with our moment in time and to find a productive way forward. She lives in San Francisco.

AMY IRVINE is a sixth-generation Utahn and longtime wilderness advocate. Her second book, *Trespass: Living at the Edge of the Promised Land*, received the Orion Book Award and Colorado Book Award—while the *Los Angeles Times* wrote that it "might very well be *Desert Solitaire*'s literary heir." Irvine teaches non-fiction in Southern New Hampshire University's MFA program and currently lives and writes in Telluride, Colorado, although her heart remains in Utah's redrock outback.

KEVIN T. JONES is an archaeologist and writer in Salt Lake City. He served as state archaeologist of Utah for seventeen years. His anthropological novel *The Shrinking Jungle* is set among the Aché, hunter-gatherers of eastern Paraguay, with whom he lived and studied as part of his dissertation research. Jones plays mandolin and sings in the bluegrass band The Lab Dogs. His favorite color is clear.

JACQUELINE KEELER is a Navajo/Yankton Dakota Sioux writer living in Portland, Oregon. She has been published in Salon.com, *Earth Island Journal*, and *The Nation*. Keeler co-founded Eradicating Offensive Native Mascotry, which seeks to end the use of racial groups as mascots. She is finishing a collection of essays called *Not Your Disappearing Indian* and editing an anthology, *Edge of Morning: Native Voices Speak for the Bears Ears*.

BROOKE LARSEN is an organizer of Uplift, a climate action community for young people across the Colorado Plateau. She worked as program coordinator at State of the Rockies after graduating from Colorado College in environmental policy and is currently studying in the University of Utah Environmental Humanities Graduate Program. She lives in Salt Lake City.

DAVID LEE, officially retired but still guest teaching, splits his time between Mesquite, Nevada; Boulder, Utah; and Seaside, Oregon, where he scribbles and wanders available trails and byways, all at about the same rate and pace. His latest book is *Bluebonnets, Firewheels, and Brown Eyed Susans: Women of Bandera 1948-1962*. He served as Utah's first poet laureate from 1997-2002 and was a finalist for United States poet laureate.

REGINA LOPEZ-WHITESKUNK was born and raised in southwestern Colorado. She has advocated for land, air, water, and animals from an early age. Lopez-Whiteskunk has traveled widely, presenting and sharing the Ute culture through song, dance, and speeches. She has served as head councilwoman of the Ute

Mountain Ute Tribe, as a member of the Colorado Commission of Indian Affairs, and as the Bears Ears Inter-Tribal Coalition co-chair. She lives in Towaoc, Colorado.

KATHLEEN DEAN MOORE is a philosopher, writer, and climate activist. Her growing alarm at the devastation of the planet led her to leave her position as Distinguished Professor at Oregon State University to speak out and to write. Her recent book, *Great Tide Rising*, follows *Moral Ground*, testimony from the world's moral leaders about our obligation to the future. Her new book is *Piano Tide*, a novel about an Alaskan village's spectacular and transformative act of resistance to the corporate plunder of their forests and streams.

GARY PAUL NABHAN is an Ecumenical Franciscan brother who works on restoring the links between biodiversity and cultural diversity. He has camped in and trekked the landscapes around the Bears Ears since working for the first Earth Day organization, Environmental Action, in 1970. He formerly served on the National Park System board appointed by Congress, and on the boards of several collaborative conservation organizations. He would sit in the W. K. Kellogg Foundation endowed chair at the University of Arizona, but he never sits down. A former nature writer and conservation biologist, he now tends an orchard in Patagonia, Arizona, and sends prayers for healing and justice out to all those who have been wounded or marginalized by divisive politics and economic disparity, in hopes for a more inclusive future.

MICHELLE NIJHUIS writes about science and the environment for *National Geographic* and other publications. She is also a longtime contributing editor of *High Country News,* a magazine known for its in-depth coverage of environmental issues in the western U.S. Her work has won national awards and been included in three *Best American* anthologies. After fifteen years off the electrical grid in rural Colorado, she and her family now live in White Salmon, Washington.

SIMON ORTIZ was raised in the Acoma Pueblo village of McCartys, New Mexico, in an Acoma-speaking family. A leading figure in the Native American literary renaissance of the 1960s, his book *Woven Stone* blends poetry and prose from three earlier volumes in a spiritual autobiography. Ortiz has received a Pushcart Prize, an NEA Fellowship, and was an honored poet at the 1981 White House Salute to Poetry. He teaches at Arizona State University.

JUAN PALMA is the former Utah State Director for the Bureau of Land Management (BLM). He led 850 employees and managed 23 million acres of BLM land in Utah. Palma began his thirty-year career in public service with the U.S. Forest Service, becoming a forest supervisor and then executive director of the Tahoe Regional Planning Agency. After serving as chief conservation officer at HECHO: Hispanics Enjoying Camping, Hunting, and the Outdoors, he now lives in Reno, where he is Nevada State Director for The Nature Conservancy.

JEN JACKSON QUINTANO made her home in the desert for a decade, finding stories and strength in the sweep of southern Utah's canyon country. Her landscape-inspired essays have been widely published, and her debut book, *Blow Sand in His Soul: Bates Wilson, the Heart of Canyonlands*, tells the story of the "father of Canyonlands National Park." She now lives with her family in Sandpoint, Idaho, where she runs an arborist business with her husband and is writing her next book.

JANA RICHMAN is the author of a memoir, *Riding in the Shadows of Saints: A Woman's Story of Motorcycling the Mormon Trail*; two novels, *The Last Cowgirl*, winner of the WILLA Award for Contemporary Fiction, and *The Ordinary Truth*; and a forthcoming collection of essays, *One Woman's Meat: Finding Stillness in a Noisy World*. Richman was born and raised in Utah's west desert, the daughter of a small-time rancher and a hand-wringing Mormon mother, and now lives in Escalante, Utah.

SAM RUSHFORTH has been a university professor and dean for more than forty-five years, teaching and researching terrestrial and aquatic biology and ecology, especially in the Great Basin and Colorado Plateau. His work has changed environmental policies and enhanced oversight through active participation in the political process and through his many committed students, now engaged in environmental and conservation work in venues across Earth. He lives in Orem, Utah.

LAURET EDITH SAVOY, a woman of African American, Euro-American, and Native American heritage, weaves together human stories of migration, displacement, and erasure that explore how this country's still unfolding history marks a person, a people, and the land itself. Her books include *Trace: Memory, History, Race, and the American Landscape*, which won the American Book Award; *The Colors of Nature: Culture, Identity and the Natural World*; and *Bedrock: Writers on the Wonders of Geology*. She is a photographer, pilot, and professor of environmental studies and geology at Mount Holyoke College.

KAREN SHEPHERD has been an activist for political, environmental, and human rights for forty-five years. She was the second woman in the history of Utah to be elected to the U.S. House of Representatives. In 1996, President Bill Clinton appointed her to represent the U.S. as director for the European Bank for Reconstruction and Development (EBRD), where she served until 2002. Shepherd has also been a fellow at the Harvard Institute of Politics and a lecturer at the University of Utah.

MARY SOJOURNER is the author of three novels: *29*, *Sisters of the Dream*, and *Going Through Ghosts*; the short story collections *Delicate* and *The Talker*; an essay collection, *Bonelight: Ruin and Grace in the New Southwest*; and the memoirs *Solace: Rituals of Loss and Desire* and *She Bets Her Life*. She lives in Flagstaff, Arizona, where she has spent three decades as an earth activist, including working to stop desecration of desecration of the sacred San Francisco Peaks.

LUCI TAPAHONSO is the inaugural Poet Laureate of the Navajo Nation and Professor Emeriti of English Languages and Literature (University of New Mexico). She is the author of three children's books and six books of poetry including *A Radiant Curve*, which was awarded the Arizona Book Award for Poetry. Tapahonso's numerous awards include the "Lifetime Achievement" award from the Native Writers Circle of the Americas and a "Spirit of the Eagle" Leadership Award for her key role in establishing the Indigenous Studies Graduate Studies Program at the University of Kansas.

ANNE TERASHIMA is from Salt Lake City, Utah, and holds a degree in English and Creative Writing from Westminster College. As associate editor and publicist at Torrey House Press, she has enjoyed nurturing the words of others by helping bring books to publication. Anne loves to hike, bike, and run in Utah's mountains and redrock. She is pursuing graduate studies at DePaul University in Chicago, Illinois.

STEPHEN TRIMBLE was a park ranger at Arches and Capitol Reef national parks in his twenties and has since published more than twenty books. He received the Sierra Club's Ansel Adams Award for photography and conservation and a Wallace Stegner Centennial Fellowship at the University of Utah Tanner Humanities Center. In 1995, Trimble co-compiled with Terry Tempest Williams the landmark book of advocacy, *Testimony: Writers of the West Speak on Behalf of Utah Wilderness*—the model for *Red Rock Stories*. He teaches writing at the University of Utah and makes his home in Salt Lake City and in Torrey, Utah.

MARK UDALL, born in Tucson, Arizona, represented the people of Colorado for sixteen years, first in the House of Representatives and then in the U.S. Senate. Before serving in Congress, Udall, an avid mountaineer, was executive director of Colorado Outward Bound. His parents, Mo and Pat Udall, shared with all their children their deep reverence for the cultural traditions, diverse communities, and landscapes of the Colorado Plateau. Udall now lives in Eldorado Springs, Colorado.

CHIP WARD drove a bookmobile, led campaigns to make polluters accountable, co-founded HEAL Utah, became the assistant director of the Salt Lake City Library System, served on the board of the Southern Utah Wilderness Alliance, and then retired to Torrey, Utah, where his journey began. His book, *Canaries on the Rim: Living Downwind in the West*, describes his political adventures in grassroots empowerment. His essays on conservation and ecological citizenship appear at Tomdispatch.com and across the web, and his novel *Stony Mesa Sagas* is forthcoming from Torrey House Press.

ANN WHITTAKER lives in Salt Lake City, Utah, where she has worked as the content manager of the online travel site Utah.com. She spent most of her childhood in Little Cottonwood Canyon and the Uinta Mountains and continues to explore Utah in depth to write its stories. Her love for literature and poetry took her to graduate school in Vermont and England with Middlebury College, where she studied the soundscape ecologies of early modern poetry.

CHARLES WILKINSON, Distinguished Professor and Moses Lasky Professor of Law at the University of Colorado, has authored or co-authored fourteen books on law, history, and society in the American West. The topics that move him the most are American Indians and the federal public lands, both central to his *Fire on the Plateau: Conflict and Endurance in the American Southwest*. Wilkinson crafted the language in President Bill Clinton's proclamation establishing Grand Staircase-Escalante National Monument.

BROOKE WILLIAMS is a partner in Tempest Exploration, LLC, whose mission is to play a role in making a quick but graceful transformation from our carbon economy to one that affirms life. He has published several books, including *Open Midnight: Where Ancestors and Wilderness Meet* and *The Story of My Heart: As Rediscovered by Brooke Williams and Terry Tempest Williams*. He lives in Castle Valley, Utah, and Moose, Wyoming.

TERRY TEMPEST WILLIAMS, writer and advocate, grew up in Salt Lake City and lives now in Castle Valley, Utah. In 1995, Williams co-compiled with Stephen Trimble the landmark book of advocacy, *Testimony: Writers of the West Speak on Behalf of Utah Wilderness*–the model for *Red Rock Stories*. Her most recent book is *The Hour of Land: A Personal Topography of America's National Parks*. With her husband, Brooke, she is redefining what energy development might mean on their 1,200-acre BLM oil and gas leases in Grand County, Utah, purchased in 2016. Williams's major honors include awards named after our wise elders, John Muir, Bob Marshall, Wallace Stegner, Rachel Carson, and John Wesley Powell. Beginning in 2017, she will be writer-in-residence at the Harvard Divinity School.

PERMISSIONS & CITATIONS

Shonto Begay
THE VIEW FROM THE MESA (in Lawana Trout, *Native American Literature: An Anthology*, McGraw Hill. Copyright © 1998 by Shonto Begay. Reprinted with permission.)

Christopher Cokinos
STONE THAT LEAPS (originally published in www.terrain.org. Reprinted with permission.)

Thomas Lowe Fleischner
THE GRACE OF WILDNESS (Adapted from: *Singing Stone: A Natural History of the Escalante Canyons*, University of Utah Press, 1999.)

Kevin Jones
THE MAN WITH A HEART OF STONE (lyrics from the song *Ancient Places* by Kevin Jones, recorded by The Lab Dogs on the album *Ancient Places*. © 2010, Howlin' Good Records, Salt Lake City.)

Simon Ortiz
RIGHT OF WAY (from *Woven Stone*. University of Arizona Press. Copyright © 1992 by Simon Ortiz. Reprinted with permission.)

Lauret Savoy
ON COMPROMISED GROUND (national park visitation statistics from Cullinane Thomas, C., and L. Koontz. 2016. 2015 National Park visitor

spending effects: Economic contributions to local communities, states, and the nation. *Natural Resource Report* NPS/NRSS/EQD/NRR–2016/1200. National Park Service, Fort Collins, Colorado. https://www.nps.gov/subjects/socialscience/vse.htm)

Luci Tapahonso
POEM (from *A Radiant Curve: Poems and Stories*, University of Arizona Press, 2008. Reprinted with permission.)

Mark Udall
WALKING TO WATER (originally published in the Grand Canyon Trust's *Colorado Plateau Advocate Magazine*, Spring/Summer 2016. Reprinted with permission.)

Terry Tempest Williams
A GESTURE OF PEACE (op-ed published July 15, 2016 in the *Salt Lake Tribune*. Reprinted with permission.)

All royalties from RED ROCK STORIES go to the Utah Wilderness Coalition, to fund grassroots organizing on behalf of Utah's redrock wilderness.

ACKNOWLEDGMENTS

ED ROCK STORIES grew from a spark, from the lifelong commitment of frontline Utah conservationists Terri Martin, Dave "Pachew" Pacheco, Diane Kelley, and Deeda Seed, who initiated our conversation in the basement of the Salt Lake City offices of the Southern Utah Wilderness Alliance. At the beginning of 2016, they created a space for the Utah writing and conservation communities to cross-pollinate. Their ongoing support and advice has been crucial.

As the conversation developed, Kirsten Johanna Allen, publisher of Torrey House Press, pushed for a "*Testimony II*," a chapbook to combat the forces of development and greed accelerating in Congress and at the Utah statehouse. Without her certainty that we needed this book, *Red Rock Stories* would not exist. Not every collaboration works; my partnership with Kirsten was a joy.

Terry Tempest Williams encouraged and challenged us early on, with strong opinions and good ideas. Ann Whittaker volunteered to create the redrockstories.org website; her energy is contagious, her taste impeccable.

Timothy Ross Lee donated his time and skills as designer for the chapbook.

We knew his work as exhibits manager and senior exhibit designer for the Natural History Museum of Utah, and we knew he could create something remarkable for this project. He did. His design captures the spirit of the redrock and lures readers into the words.

We raised money for the chapbook from individuals. This trade edition for general readers, with additional material, attracted financial support from foundations and conservation groups.

We thank: Tom and Laura Bacon, Tom and Lydia Berggren, Jason Corzine, John and Lee Diamond, Paula and Gary Evershed, Carolyn Gray and George Peppard, Jennifer Jordan, Marty Krasney, Kathleen and Peter Metcalf, and Jennifer Speers. Major contributions from the Southern Utah Wilderness Alliance, led by Scott Groene; the Utah Chapter of The Nature Conservancy, led by Dave Livermore; and The Wilderness Society, with thanks to Soren Jespersen and Scott Miller, supported this trade edition. Thanks to them all for their generosity and vision.

When we placed the call for pieces from writers, Charles Wilkinson helped immensely. His connections to tribal people and to the Bears Ears Inter-Tribal Coalition brought critical Native voices into our book.

181

His deep knowledge of Indian and public lands law made him the perfect person to write our introductory essay. Charles's graciousness and tenacity propelled both the book and the monument.

In June 2016, Kirsten Allen and I took the book to decision makers in Washington, D.C. Jen Ujifusa of the Southern Utah Wilderness Alliance was our key advisor. Many thanks to her for patiently helping us negotiate the labyrinths of government, and, especially, for setting up our press conference. Regina Lopez-Whiteskunk's eloquence that day animated the windowless Edward R. Murrow Room at the National Press Club with the spiritual connection Native people sustain with this land.

Special thanks to Bruce Babbitt, who kindly wrote our cover letter when we distributed the book to members of Congress, lending us the credibility and seriousness associated with his name. Thanks to the champions of redrock wilderness in Congress, especially Representative Alan Lowenthal and Senators Dick Durbin and Martin Heinrich.

The staff members of the tiny but mighty Torrey House Press have worked tirelessly to place this book in your hands: Kirsten Allen, Alisha Anderson, Mark Bailey, Brooke Larsen, and Anne Terashima.

Thanks to you all for a dedicated group effort on behalf of the land.

S.T.

RED ROCK HISTORY

LETTER FROM BEARS EARS
INTER-TRIBAL COALITION

The leaders of the Bears Ears Inter-Tribal Coalition met in good faith for three years with the stakeholders of the Public Lands Initiative. Their proposals built on two-and-a-half years of work with tribal elders to identify and map sacred sites and cultural connections in southeastern Utah. When the Coalition leaders reluctantly concluded their voices could not be heard, they sent this letter to Utah Congressional Representatives Jason Chaffetz and Rob Bishop on December 31, 2015.

BEARS EARS INTER-TRIBAL COALITION
A Partnership of the Hopi, Navajo, Uintah & Ouray Ute,
Ute Mountain Ute, and Zuni Governments

December 31, 2015

Hon. Rob Bishop
Hon. Jason Chaffetz
U.S. House of Representatives
Washington, D.C. 20515

RE: Status of the Bears Ears Coalition-PLI Discussions

Dear Representatives Bishop and Chaffetz:

The Coalition held a day-long meeting on December 30, 2015, at
the White Mesa Tribal Headquarters. Most of the meeting con-
sisted of a full-scale review and evaluation of the discussions
with PLI. These are the results of our deliberations.

On July 16, 2015, the Coalition, knowing that it would be ex-
tremely difficult, set a firm deadline of October 15 for submitting to President Obama and the PLI a comprehensive proposal
for a Bears Ears National Monument. After an intensive series
of well-attended drafting meetings, we met that deadline. In discussing what steps we should take next, we considered whether we should first negotiate with the PLI to see if congressional
action might make it unnecessary for the President to declare

a monument under the Antiquities Act. We concluded that we should meet with the PLI first and resolved to make our best effort to achieve a satisfactory congressional resolution.

In doing so, we are very conscious of our obligations to our ancestors. The events leading up to our proposal of October 15, 2015, have been long in the making. Ever since the 1800s, when all Indian people residing in the Bears Ears area were forcibly removed, we have grieved and suffered great pain over the treatment of these ancestral lands. The looting and grave robbing has been extensive, despicable, and continuous. Irresponsible mining and off-road vehicle use have torn up the ground. These and other actions have violated and despoiled our ancestors' homes and other structures. Generations of misuse and other bad conduct have interfered with, and sometimes nearly destroyed, our gathering of medicines and herbs, sacred ceremonies, family gatherings, and individual prayers and offerings, all the things that heal us and the land. But our people revere the Bears Ears area, and we continue to visit it in spite of the conduct of others because for us it remains a special place, where we can be among our ancestors and their songs and wisdom, where the traumas of the past can be alleviated, where we can connect with the land and our deepest values and heal.

We were very apprehensive about entering into discussions with the PLI. Up to that time, the PLI had never taken us seriously. This was in spite of the fact that we worked tirelessly on the PLI process, putting in as much or more effort as any party involved in the process. We made at least 25 presentations at PLI meetings, complete with maps, a two-page summary of the UDB proposal (the precursor to the pending Coalition proposal), and substantial oral presentations. Congressional staff was present at approximately a dozen of these meetings. We also made eight separate trips to Washington, D.C. to meet with the Utah delegation; at each of those meetings, we made extensive statements complete with maps and a summary of the proposal. At all of these meetings, both in the field and in Washington, D.C., we asked for comments on our proposal. Our extensive and unwavering efforts to engage in the PLI process are cataloged in great detail in Exhibit One of our proposal.

It was to no avail. In no instance did anyone from the Utah delegation or the PLI make a single substantive comment, positively or negatively, on our proposal.

Our painful experience with attempting to make an inroad into the PLI process was epitomized by our dealings with the San Juan County Commission. Although the proponents of the PLI described the process as "open" and "ground-up," PLI leaders said that they were relying heavily on county commissions. We were repeatedly told to present our proposal to the San Juan County commission.

The San Juan County Commission conducted a public comment process on PLI in 2014. The UDB proposal was identified as "Alternative D." Commission staff agreed to include Alternative D in the list of alternatives. Then the staff changed that commitment and refused to include Alternative D on the list.

Supporters of Alternative D waged a write-in campaign. Despite being omitted from the list, Alternative D received 300 positive comments, 64% of the 467 total comments received. The Commission then completely rejected the results of its own survey-and the wishes of the Indian people who comprise 53% of the population of San Juan County-and selected the heavy-development, low conservation "Alternative B." Alternative B had received just two comments, one half of 1% of the total.

In spite of the extraordinary unfairness of this proceeding—the kind of raw, heavy-handed political overreaching rarely seen in America today—at no time has San Juan County, the PLI, or the Utah delegation ever seen fit to acknowledge it, much less apologize and disown it.

Because of the frustration and resentment caused by this long progression of events, the Native people supporting protection for Bears Ears requested the sovereign Indian nations to take the lead in requesting action from President Obama and attempting to obtain satisfactory legislation from the PLI process. Our five sovereign Indian nations, the Hopi, Navajo, Uintah & Ouray Ute, Ute Mountain Ute, and Zuni then formally created the Bears Ears Inter-Tribal Coalition in July 2015.

Despite all of the past difficulties, after the completion of our proposal on October 15 we entered into these discussions with PLI with open minds. Two meetings have been held, on October 29 at the Ute Mountain Ute Tribal Headquarters in Towaoc and on November 30 on Capitol Hill in Washington, D.C. Both meetings were characterized by civil discourse. There was, however, almost nothing substantive from the PLI side. We asked several times for reactions, positive or negative, to our proposal but received no substantive responses. The closest was the statement by a PLI staff member at the Towaoc meeting that "we like the idea of cooperative management." Cooperative management, however, is a broad term with many applications and definitions. Our proposal calls for a strong and unique definition of collaborative management that the staff did not comment on.

At the Coalition meeting on December 30, we reflected on the two recent meetings and realized that they fit into the pattern that we have long experienced with the PLI. At the public meetings on the PLI, the moderators, including the Congressmen,were always polite. When we went back to Washington, D.C. in 2013-2015 for our eight meetings with the Utah delegation and staff, everyone was polite and friendly. They were pleasant meetings. But they offered no substantive engagement at all. The same was true with our recent meetings in Towaoc and Washington, D.C. Despite our inquiries, PLI representatives had nothing to say about the proposal that we had so painstakingly developed. Once again, we were not being taken seriously.

This was all underscored by the events directly leading up to our recent December 30 Coalition meeting. That day was not supposed to be a Coalition meeting.

At the end of the November 30, 2015, meeting in Washington, D.C., both sides talked about the next meeting date; we all agreed that December 30 was a most promising date and that we would all check our calendars. For us, this was late: it was a month away, and from the beginning we had made it clear—and PLI staffers agreed—that time was of the essence. Still, we were willing to do it.

On December 15, 2015, PLI staff advised us that Congressman Chaffetz would be unable to attend a meeting on December 30. We promptly responded with our regrets but asked for confirmation that the staff would still be able to meet on December 30. A week later, on December 23, a lead staffer responded that he would be unable to attend the December 30 meeting and we were advised on December 29 that the other staffers could not attend.

These cancellations complicated matters for us considerably. Needless to say, December 30 was not a convenient date for us, but we all had set it aside because of the importance of these negotiations.

In addition, we were shocked by the staff's December 23 email. At the October 29 meeting in Towaoc, the PLI representatives assured us that a PLI draft would be available soon, perhaps as early as November. That did not occur. Then, at the November 30 meeting in Washington, D.C., PLI staff "guaranteed" that we would receive the PLI draft before December 30. But, to our surprise, on December 23, PLI staff advised us that the promised draft PLI would not be available on December 30. We had depended upon receiving the draft PLI so that we would have a basis for determining the thrust of the PLI's view of our proposal. Now, after 2 1/2 months since providing them with our proposal on the date promised, we had not received a single reaction to it. On December 24, Tribal Leaders convened a conference call to discuss options including discontinuation of discussions with PLI.

Coalition members then spent December 30 discussing in detail the state of the negotiations with PLI from beginning to end.

We have come to the conclusion that we have no choice but to discontinue these discussions. Our strenuous efforts to participate in the PLI, and related proceedings before that over the course of the past six years, have been consistently stonewalled. We have never been taken seriously. Now, 2 1/2 months after submitting our proposal to you, we have received no reactions at all from you on our proposal. The promised draft PLI was never delivered. All of this is consistent with PLI's repeated failures to meet deadlines. Our five sovereign tribal nations, and our carefully-drafted comprehensive proposal, deserve far more than that.

Again, time is of the essence. We don't feel we can wait any longer before engaging with the Obama Administration concerning our proposal in the hope that they will advance our proposal via the Antiquities Act. If, at some point, you decide to submit to us a comprehensive proposal for what you specifically intend to include in the PLI legislation and process, including a firm date for passage by Congress, then we will promptly review that submission and advise you as to whether it would be worthwhile for us to re-establish discussions. In the meantime, we have no choice but to turn our attention to working with the Obama Administration.

Respectfully,

ERIC DESCHEENIE
Co-Chair
Bears Ears Inter-Tribal Coalition

ALFRED LOMAHQUAHU
Co-Chair
Bears Ears Inter-Tribal Coalition

LETTER OF INVITATION TO CONTRIBUTORS

Writers have a long tradition of work in service to conservation in Utah and the West. Fully aware of acting within this tradition and with the model of the 1995 collection, *Testimony*, Kirsten Allen and I sent the following letter of invitation to contributors on April 8, 2016.

April 8, 2016

Dear friends:

Twenty years ago, Terry Tempest Williams and I asked Western writers to speak on behalf of Utah wilderness. A terrible bill in Congress threatened to remove protection from millions of acres of astonishing landscapes, and we believed that the voices of writers would make a difference. Twenty passionate and well-crafted responses came together in the book, *Testimony*, piercing the hearts of decision makers, who listened. The book had power and consequence.

It's again time to ask for your help. Threats to wild Utah have accelerated, bringing us to a point of crisis and opportunity. We respond as writers—taking full advantage of twenty-first-century media. We write with an awareness of our fragile future, not just as "nature writers" but as citizens connected to global grassroots movements seeking environmental and climate justice.

Current threats take aim at every cherished Utah landscape and the foundational principles of America's public lands. The Utah congressional delegation again has written a dangerous bill, the Public Lands Initiative (PLI). The PLI legislation could arrive on the desks of members of Congress at any time—along with other bills attacking the integrity of our public lands. The Utah state legislature continues to insist that "we the people" turn over nearly all of Utah's federal lands for ownership and development by the state. Relentless local officials, eager to wreak havoc on the integrity of wildlands, claim ownership of thousands of miles of "roads" that are in reality little more than cow paths. The media grants a bully pulpit to Cliven Bundy and his gang, holed up in armed camps at Bunkerville and Malheur, and not everyone dismisses their rants.

First in the lineup of legislation that shreds protection for remaining Utah wildlands, the PLI opens up vast territory to destruction by the fossil fuel industry. Representative Rob Bishop announced the PLI process by asking for a "grand bargain," pledging to resolve public land issues through conversation and compromise among all factions, from Dinosaur National Monument and the Uintas south to San Juan County and the Bears Ears. Instead, he turned to industry and rural county commissioners for final say on the bill's content. Never before has a single bill included so many unprecedented exceptions to the Wilderness Act, undermining the nation's historic promise to preserve untrammeled land. This may be the worst public lands bill ever.

The Bears Ears Inter-Tribal Coalition counters such arrogance with an extraordinary proposal supported by twenty-six tribes. They've asked President Obama to create a new national monument to preserve the land sweeping south from Canyonlands National Park to the Navajo Nation.

The president needs our supportive words if he is to preserve the Bears Ears. As writers tied to this place, our voices, straight from our hearts, will form the bedrock of a multi-generational celebration of the spirit of Utah wilderness and a rallying cry for activists working to keep fossil fuels in the ground, where that carbon belongs.

And so, we invite you to donate a short piece of writing, to participate in the community project we're calling *Red Rock Stories*. We'll anchor this initiative with a limited-edition chapbook. The nonprofit Torrey House Press will help with logistics and follow the chapbook with a trade edition, with royalties going to the

Utah Wilderness Coalition. A Red Rock Stories website will build on this core content with podcasts, videos, photographs, readings, and interviews.

Send us the most moving, most impassioned, most carefully argued words you have ever crafted in the name of wildness. This may be a fragment, a paragraph, a poem, an excerpt, or an essay. Please write no more than 800 words. You'll retain copyright, of course, but we are asking your permission to allow *Red Rock Stories* to use your words in every way we can think of to further the cause of Wild Utah.

Before the current congress recesses in mid-July, we will design and bind a Red Rock Stories chapbook. We'll rely on advice from the conservation community to organize distribution in Washington, D.C. We're pursuing funding for publication costs.

We write in the lineage that begins with Wallace Stegner's *Wilderness Letter* and *This Is Dinosaur.* We believe in writing as an act of faith. We know that you will use your skills to speak to the irreplaceable spiritual, cultural, and ecological values of Utah wilderness.

If you choose a specific setting for your piece, consider choosing one of these endangered and lesser-known jewels if you know them. In the Bears Ears and PLI: White Canyon, Tables of the Sun (south of Highway 95), Hatch Point/Canyon Rims, and Nokai Dome. Beyond the Bears Ears but still in the PLI: Labyrinth Canyon, Desolation Canyon, southern Book Cliffs, and the San Rafael Swell (especially the western end). Nearby public lands just as worthy: the Dirty Devil wilderness and the Henry Mountains.

We need your piece no later than May 6th. We know this is an inconsiderate and demanding request, but stakes are high and the timeline is tight. In order to have your words be fully present in the Bears Ears conversation, we need to deliver this collection to Congress by early July.

Thank you for your good work, for your lifetimes of fine writing and engaged citizenship,

Steve

Stephen Trimble

Kristen

Kirsten Johanna Allen,
for Torrey House Press

from
TESTIMONY: WRITERS OF THE WEST
SPEAK ON BEHALF OF UTAH WILDERNESS (1995)

"...in wilderness, as in the eyes of the wild creatures that inhabit it, we find something that binds us firmly to the long history of life on earth, something that can teach us how to live on this cooling cinder of a planet, how to accept our limitations, how to celebrate the love we feel when we let ourselves feel it for all other living creatures."

T.H. WATKINS
(1936-2000)

"You could listen to those with a frontier hangover so great, they still reject any notion of limits, or you can heed the enlightened consensus of ecological sanity and a hunger for wild places. ...We cannot measure this land with numbers or dollars. It looks so very peculiar, like red bones. But we need this strangely wild country, for here we can explore and rest and listen in an agreed peace."

ELLEN MELOY
(1946-2004)

LETTER ACCOMPANYING
RED ROCK TESTIMONY CHAPBOOK

When we distributed a copy of the chapbook in early July 2016 to every member of the United States Congress, we knew the book would attract maximum attention if we included a cover letter from a person of stature. Bruce Babbitt agreed to write this letter, which we reproduce here (in its Senate version)

July 5, 2016

Dear members of the United States Senate:

Today we have the good fortune to send you an important and unusual collection of essays and poems that speak to the spiritual, cultural, and scientific values of Utah's canyon country. This isn't your standard Congressional testimony filled with bureaucratese and charts. This privately-published limited edition book gathers impassioned "Red Rock Testimony" from prominent American writers whose backgrounds span generations and geography, race, and culture. I'm honored to be one of these writers.

The book opens with an introduction by Charles Wilkinson, the preeminent scholar of public lands and Indian law. Contributors include Navajo Poet Laureate Luci Tapahonso and Utah's first poet laureate David Lee, MacArthur Fellow Gary Paul Nabhan, writer-philosopher Kathleen Dean Moore, former Utah state archaeologist Kevin Jones, Ute Mountain Ute tribal councilwoman Regina Lopez-Whiteskunk, former members of Congress Mark Udall and Karen Shepherd, bestselling essayists David Gessner and Lauret Savoy, recent Utah Bureau of Land Management director Juan Palma, and award-winning writer-scholars who teach at universities from North Carolina to Arizona.

These 34 writers explore the fierce beauty and the threats to ecological and archaeological integrity that define the issues in this politically embattled corner of our country. The writers and designer of *Red Rock Testimony* donated their work for this chapbook, with printing funded by individual contributions from Utah citizens. Just 1500 copies were printed.

As the Utah delegation considers introducing public lands legislation and as the Administration considers the establishment of a Bears Ears National Monument, this is an important book to review. Please read, enjoy, and contemplate this literary gift to the conversation. These dedicated writers will transport you to the wild beauty of the canyon country I love and, we hope, encourage you to join us in support of preserving the magnificent landscapes that inspire these moving words.

Sincerely,

BRUCE BABBITT

INTRODUCTION TO THE PROCLAMATION

President Obama and his administration welcomed the idea of creating a national monument dedicated to Indian culture. Yet new ideas, however compelling, come with risks. As 2016 ticked away, there were many discussions and much research but few decisions in the Interior and Agriculture buildings in Washington, D.C.

The president believed in using the Antiquities Act to protect land only after Congress failed to act. As long as there was any chance of PLI passage, the Obama administration was determined to wait.

A turning point emerged when Interior Secretary Sally Jewell came to Utah with agency and department officials to see the Bears Ears landscape and meet with all sides. She presided over an extraordinary 3 ½-hour public hearing in Bluff on July 16, 2016, that drew more than 2,000 people, a number rarely seen at such events. A clear majority of the crowd—at least half of them Native American—favored a national monument. Their testimony embodied the beauty and dignity of the Indian way.

As Secretary Jewell and her colleagues made their way back to Washington, they surely must have felt a growing conviction that Bears Ears fully deserved to be protected as a monument and managed under a regime that gave Indian people a prominent voice in managing that landscape.

By early December, the PLI was officially dead. In the House, it had gone through committee but never made it to the floor. The bill was never introduced in the Senate. Now was the time for President Obama to make his final decision.

The president long had an ambitious vision in mind. He sent a message into one early planning meeting, challenging federal and tribal representatives to come up with "something bold and new."

With the research and analysis complete, the president decided to create a national monument. The agencies formed a drafting committee and presented the President with a formal proclamation, which he signed on December 28, 2016.

The Bears Ears proclamation calls for a new kind of national monument, presenting Indian culture and traditions in as realistic and uplifting a fashion as any federal document ever has. And yet, following the change in administrations in January 2017, Utah politicians began campaigning to eviscerate or eliminate the new monument.

The lessons of history and the needs and opportunities of the future point in a different direction. The purpose of the Bears Ears proclamation is to honor the tribes who have walked the Bears Ears landscape and to honor their relationship with this landscape. The proclamation elevates traditional knowledge to the status of "a resource to be protected and used in understanding and managing this landscape." The promise of the monument lies in this creative and vigorous fusion of traditional knowledge and western land management practices.

In the Bears Ears proclamation's vivid and visionary descriptions of Indian culture and traditional knowledge, and in beautifully written accounts of the wonder of this rare, elegant place, the president's challenge has been met.

CHARLES WILKINSON

PROCLAMATION OF BEARS EARS NATIONAL MONUMENT

BY PRESIDENT BARACK OBAMA

December 28, 2016

ESTABLISHMENT OF THE BEARS EARS NATIONAL MONUMENT

BY THE PRESIDENT OF THE UNITED STATES OF AMERICA

A PROCLAMATION

Rising from the center of the southeastern Utah landscape and visible from every direction are twin buttes so distinctive that in each of the native languages of the region their name is the same: Hoon'Naqvut, Shash Jáa, Kwiyagatu Nukavachi, Ansh An Lashokdiwe, or "Bears Ears." For hundreds of generations, native peoples lived in the surrounding deep sandstone canyons, desert mesas, and meadow mountaintops, which constitute one of the densest and most significant cultural landscapes in the United States. Abundant rock art, ancient cliff dwellings, ceremonial sites, and countless other artifacts provide an extraordinary archaeological and cultural record that is important to us all, but most notably the land is profoundly sacred to many Native American tribes, including the Ute Mountain Ute Tribe, Navajo Nation, Ute Indian Tribe of the Uintah Ouray, Hopi Nation, and Zuni Tribe.

Ancestral Puebloans followed, beginning to occupy the area at least 2,500 years ago, leaving behind items from their daily life such as baskets, pottery, and weapons. These early farmers of Basketmaker II, and III and builders of Pueblo I, II and III left their marks on the land. The remains of single family dwellings, granaries, kivas, towers, and large villages and roads linking them together reveal a complex cultural history. "Moki steps," hand and toe holds carved into steep canyon walls by the Ancestral Puebloans, illustrate the early people's ingenuity and perseverance and are still used today to access dwellings along cliff walls. Other, distinct cultures have thrived here as well – the Fremont People, Numic- and Athabaskan-speaking hunter-gatherers, and Utes and Navajos. Resources such as the Doll House Ruin in Dark Canyon Wilderness Area and the Moon House Ruin on Cedar Mesa allow visitors to marvel at artistry and architecture that have withstood thousands of seasons in this harsh climate.

The landscape is a milieu of the accessible and observable together with the inaccessible and hidden. The area's petroglyphs and pictographs capture the imagination with images dating back at least 5,000 years and spanning a range of styles and traditions. From life-size ghostlike figures that defy categorization, to the more literal depictions of bighorn sheep, birds, and lizards, these drawings enable us to feel the humanity of these ancient artists. The Indian Creek area contains spectacular rock art, including hundreds of petroglyphs at Newspaper Rock. Visitors to Bears Ears can also discover more recent rock art left by the Ute, Navajo, and Paiute peoples. It is also the less visible sites, however – those that supported the food gathering, subsistence and ceremony of daily life – that tell the story of the people who lived here. Historic remnants of Native American sheep-herding and farming are scattered throughout the area, and pottery and Navajo hogans record the lifeways of native peoples in the 19th and 20th centuries.

For thousands of years, humans have occupied and stewarded this land. With respect to most of these people, their contribution to the historical record is unknown, but some have played a more public role. Famed Navajo headman K'aayélii was born around 1800 near the twin Bears Ears buttes. His band used the area's remote canyons to elude capture by the U.S. Army and avoid the fate that befell many other Navajo bands: surrender, the Long Walk, and forced relocation to Bosque Redondo. Another renowned 19th century Navajo leader, "Hastiin Ch'ihaajin" Manuelito, was also born near the Bears Ears.

The area's cultural importance to Native American tribes continues to this day. As they have for generations, these tribes and their members come here for ceremonies and to visit sacred sites. Throughout the region, many landscape features, such as Comb Ridge, the San Juan River, and Cedar Mesa, are closely tied to native stories of creation, danger, protection, and healing. The towering spires in the Valley of the Gods are sacred to the Navajo, representing ancient Navajo warriors frozen in stone. Traditions of hunting, fishing, gathering, and wood cutting are still practiced by tribal members, as is collection of medicinal and ceremonial plants, edible herbs, and materials for crafting items like baskets and footwear. The traditional ecological knowledge amassed by the Native Americans whose ancestors inhabited this region, passed down from generation to generation, offers critical insight into the historic and scientific significance of the area. Such knowledge is, itself, a resource to be protected and used in understanding and managing this landscape sustainably for generations to come.

Euro-Americans first explored the Bears Ears area during the 18th century, and Mormon settlers followed in the late 19th century. The San Juan Mission expedition traversed this rugged country in 1880 on their journey to establish a new settlement in what is now Bluff, Utah. To ease the passage of wagons over the slick rock slopes and through the canyonlands, the settlers smoothed sections of the rock surface and constructed dugways and other features still visible along their route, known as the Hole-in-the-Rock Trail. Cabins, corrals, trails, and carved inscriptions in the rock reveal the lives of ranchers, prospectors, and early archaeologists. Cattle rustlers and other outlaws created a convoluted trail network known as the Outlaw Trail, said to be used by Butch Cassidy and the Sundance Kid. These outlaws took advantage of the area's network of canyons, including the aptly-named Hideout Canyon, to avoid detection.

The area's stunning geology, from sharp pinnacles to broad mesas, labyrinthine canyons to solitary hoodoos, and verdant hanging gardens to bare stone arches and natural bridges, provides vital insights to geologists. In the east, the Abajo Mountains tower, reaching elevations of more than 11,000 feet. A long geologic history is documented in the colorful rock layers visible in the area's canyons.

For long periods over 300 million years ago, these lands were inundated by tropical seas and hosted thriving coral reefs. These seas infused the area's black rock shale with salts as they receded. Later, the lands were bucked upwards multiple times by the Monument Upwarp, and near-volcanoes punched up through the rock, leaving their marks on the landscape without reaching the surface. In the sandstone of Cedar Mesa, fossil evidence has revealed large, mammal-like reptiles that burrowed into the sand to survive the blistering heat of the end of the Permian Period, when the region was dominated by a seaside desert. Later, in the Late Triassic Period more than 200 million years ago, seasonal monsoons flooded an ancient river system that fed a vast desert here.

The paleontological resources in the Bears Ears area are among the richest and most significant in the United States, and protection of this area will provide important opportunities for further archaeological and paleontological study. Many sites, such as Arch Canyon, are teeming with fossils, and research conducted in the Bears Ears area is revealing new insights into the transition of vertebrate life from reptiles to mammals and from sea to land. Numerous ray-finned fish fossils from the Permian Period have been discovered, along with other late Paleozoic Era fossils, including giant amphibians, synapsid reptiles, and important plant fossils. Fossilized traces of marine and aquatic creatures such as clams, crayfish, fish, and aquatic reptiles have been found in Indian Creek's Chinle Formation, dating to the Triassic Period, and phytosaur and dinosaur fossils from the same period have been found along Comb Ridge. Paleontologists have identified new species of plant-eating crocodile-like reptiles and mass graves of lumbering sauropods, along with metoposaurus, crocodiles, and other dinosaur fossils. Fossilized trackways of early tetrapods can be seen in the Valley of the Gods and in Indian Creek, where paleontologists have also discovered exceptional examples of fossilized ferns, horsetails, and cycads. The Chinle Formation and the Wingate, Kayenta, and Navajo Formations above it provide one of the best continuous rock records of the Triassic-Jurassic transition in the world, crucial to understanding how dinosaurs dominated terrestrial ecosystems and how our mammalian ancestors evolved. In Pleistocene Epoch sediments, scientists have found traces of mammoths, short-faced bears, ground sloths, primates, and camels.

From earth to sky, the region is unsurpassed in wonders. The star-filled nights and natural quiet of the Bears Ears area transport visitors to an earlier eon. Against an absolutely black night sky, our galaxy and others more distant leap into view. As one of the most intact and least roaded areas in the contiguous United States, Bears Ears has that rare and arresting quality of deafening silence.

Communities have depended on the resources of the region for hundreds of generations. Understanding the important role of the green highlands in providing habitat for subsistence plants and animals, as well as capturing and filtering water from passing storms, the Navajo refer to such places as "Nahodishgish," or places to be left alone. Local communities seeking to protect the mountains for their watershed values have long recognized the importance of the Bears Ears' headwaters. Wildfires, both natural and human-set, have shaped and maintained forests and grasslands of this area for millennia. Ranchers have relied on the forests and grasslands of the region for ages, and hunters come from across the globe for a chance at a bull elk or other big game. Today, ecological restoration through the careful use of wildfire and management of grazing and timber is working to restore and maintain the health of these vital watersheds and grasslands.

The diversity of the soils and microenvironments in the Bears Ears area provide habitat for a wide variety of vegetation. The highest elevations, in the Elk Ridge area of the Manti-La Sal National Forest, contain pockets of ancient Engelmann spruce, ponderosa pine, aspen, and subalpine fir. Mesa tops include pinyon-juniper woodlands along with big sagebrush, low sage, blackbrush, rabbitbrush, bitterbrush, four-wing saltbush, shadscale, winterfat, Utah serviceberry, western chokecherry, hackberry, barberry, cliff rose, and greasewood. Canyons contain diverse vegetation ranging from yucca and cacti such as prickly pear, claret cup, and Whipple's fishhook to mountain mahogany, ponderosa pine, alder, sagebrush, birch, dogwood, and Gambel's oak, along with occasional stands of aspen. Grasses and herbaceous species such as bluegrass, bluestem, giant ryegrass, ricegrass, needle and thread, yarrow, common mallow, balsamroot, low larkspur, horsetail, and peppergrass also grow here, as well as pinnate spring parsley, Navajo penstemon, Canyonlands lomatium, and the Abajo daisy.

Tucked into winding canyons are vibrant riparian communities characterized by Fremont cottonwood, western sandbar willow, yellow willow, and box elder. Numerous seeps provide year-round water and support delicate hanging gardens, moisture-loving plants, and relict species such as Douglas fir. A few populations of the rare Kachina daisy, endemic to the Colorado Plateau, hide in shaded seeps and alcoves of the area's canyons. A genetically distinct population of Kachina daisy was also found on Elk Ridge. The alcove columbine and cave primrose, also regionally endemic, grow in seeps and hanging gardens in the Bears Ears landscape. Wildflowers such as beardtongue, evening primrose, aster, Indian paintbrush, yellow and purple beeflower, straight bladderpod, Durango tumble mustard, scarlet gilia, globe mallow, sand verbena, sego lily, cliffrose, sacred datura, monkey flower, sunflower, prince's plume, hedgehog cactus, and columbine, bring bursts of color to the landscape.

The diverse vegetation and topography of the Bears Ears area, in turn, support a variety of wildlife species. Mule deer and elk range on the mesas and near canyon heads, which provide crucial habitat for both species. The Cedar Mesa landscape is home to bighorn sheep which were once abundant but still live in Indian Creek, and in the canyons north of the San Juan River. Small mammals such as desert cottontail, black-tailed jackrabbit, prairie dog, Botta's pocket gopher, white-tailed antelope squirrel, Colorado chipmunk, canyon mouse, deer mouse, pinyon mouse, and desert woodrat, as well as Utah's only population of Abert's tassel-eared squirrels, find shelter and sustenance in the landscape's canyons and uplands. Rare shrews, including a variant of Merriam's shrew and the dwarf shrew can be found in this area.

Carnivores, including badger, coyote, striped skunk, ringtail, gray fox, bobcat, and the occasional mountain lion, all hunt here, while porcupines use their sharp quills and climbing abilities to escape these predators. Oral histories from the Ute describe the historic presence of bison, antelope, and abundant bighorn sheep, which are also depicted in ancient rock art. Black bear pass through the area but are rarely seen, though they are common in the oral histories and legends of this region, including those of the Navajo.

Consistent sources of water in a dry landscape draw diverse wildlife species to the area's riparian habitats, including an array of amphibian species such as tiger salamander, red-spotted toad, Woodhouse's toad, canyon tree frog, Great Basin spadefoot, and northern leopard frog. Even the most sharp-eyed visitors probably will not catch a glimpse of the secretive Utah night lizard.

Other reptiles in the area include the sagebrush lizard, eastern fence lizard, tree lizard, side-blotched lizard, plateau striped whiptail, western rattlesnake, night snake, striped whipsnake, and gopher snake.

Raptors such as the golden eagle, peregrine falcon, bald eagle, northern harrier, northern goshawk, red-tailed hawk, ferruginous hawk, American kestrel, flammulated owl, and great horned owl hunt their prey on the mesa tops with deadly speed and accuracy. The largest contiguous critical habitat for the threatened Mexican spotted owl is on the Manti-La Sal National Forest. Other bird species found in the area include Merriam's turkey, Williamson's sapsucker, common nighthawk, white-throated swift, ash-throated flycatcher, violet-green swallow, cliff swallow, mourning dove, pinyon jay, sagebrush sparrow, canyon towhee, rock wren, sage thrasher, and the endangered southwestern willow flycatcher.

As the skies darken in the evenings, visitors may catch a glimpse of some the area's at least 15 species of bats, including the big free-tailed bat, pallid bat, Townsend's big-eared bat, spotted bat, and silver-haired bat. Tinajas, rock depressions filled with rainwater, provide habitat for many specialized aquatic species, including pothole beetles and freshwater shrimp. Eucosma navajoensis, an endemic moth that has only been described near Valley of the Gods, is unique to this area.

Protection of the Bears Ears area will preserve its cultural, prehistoric, and historic legacy and maintain its diverse array of natural and scientific resources, ensuring that the prehistoric, historic, and scientific values of this area remain for the benefit of all Americans. The Bears Ears area has been proposed for protection by members of Congress, Secretaries of the Interior, State and tribal leaders, and local conservationists for at least 80 years. The area contains numerous objects of historic and of scientific interest, and it provides world class outdoor recreation opportunities, including rock climbing, hunting, hiking, backpacking, canyoneering, whitewater rafting, mountain biking, and horseback riding. Because visitors travel from near and far, these lands support a growing travel and tourism sector that is a source of economic opportunity for the region.

WHEREAS, section 320301 of title 54, United States Code (known as the "Antiquities Act"), authorizes the President, in his discretion, to declare by public proclamation historic landmarks, historic and prehistoric structures, and other objects of historic or scientific interest that are situated upon the lands owned or controlled by the Federal Government to be national monuments, and to reserve as a part thereof parcels of land, the limits of which shall be confined to the smallest area compatible with the proper care and management of the objects to be protected;

WHEREAS, it is in the public interest to preserve the objects of scientific and historic interest on the Bears Ears lands;

NOW, THEREFORE, I, BARACK OBAMA, President of the United States of America, by the authority vested in me by section 320301 of title 54, United States Code, hereby proclaim the objects identified above that are situated upon lands and interests in lands owned or controlled by the Federal Government to be the Bears Ears National Monument (monument) and, for the purpose of protecting those objects, reserve as part thereof all lands and interests in lands owned or controlled by the Federal Government within the boundaries described on the accompanying map, which is attached to and forms a part of this proclamation. These reserved Federal lands and interests in lands encompass approximately 1.35 million acres. The boundaries described on the accompanying map are confined to the smallest area compatible with the proper care and management of the objects to be protected.

All Federal lands and interests in lands within the boundaries of the monument are hereby appropriated and withdrawn from all forms of entry, location, selection, sale, or other disposition under the public land laws or laws applicable to the U.S. Forest

Service, from location, entry, and patent under the mining laws, and from disposition under all laws relating to mineral and geothermal leasing, other than by exchange that furthers the protective purposes of the monument.

The establishment of the monument is subject to valid existing rights, including valid existing water rights. If the Federal Government acquires ownership or control of any lands or interests in lands that it did not previously own or control within the boundaries described on the accompanying map, such lands and interests in lands shall be reserved as a part of the monument, and objects identified above that are situated upon those lands and interests in lands shall be part of the monument, upon acquisition of ownership or control by the Federal Government.

The Secretary of Agriculture and the Secretary of the Interior (Secretaries) shall manage the monument through the U.S. Forest Service (USFS) and the Bureau of Land Management (BLM), pursuant to their respective applicable legal authorities, to implement the purposes of this proclamation. The USFS shall manage that portion of the monument within the boundaries of the National Forest System (NFS), and the BLM shall manage the remainder of the monument. The lands administered by the USFS shall be managed as part of the Manti-La Sal National Forest. The lands administered by the BLM shall be managed as a unit of the National Landscape Conservation System, pursuant to applicable legal authorities.

For purposes of protecting and restoring the objects identified above, the Secretaries shall jointly prepare a management plan for the monument and shall promulgate such regulations for its management as they deem appropriate. The Secretaries, through the USFS and the BLM, shall consult with other Federal land management agencies in the local area, including the National Park Service, in developing the management plan. In promulgating any management rules and regulations governing the NFS lands within the monument and developing the management plan, the Secretary of Agriculture, through the USFS, shall consult with the Secretary of the Interior through the BLM. The Secretaries shall provide for maximum public involvement in the development of that plan including, but not limited to, consultation with federally recognized tribes and State and local governments. In the development and implementation of the management plan, the Secretaries shall maximize opportunities, pursuant to applicable legal authorities, for shared resources, operational efficiency, and cooperation.

The Secretaries, through the BLM and USFS, shall establish an advisory committee under the Federal Advisory Committee Act (5 U.S.C. App.) to provide information and advice regarding the development of the management plan and, as appropriate, management of the monument. This advisory committee shall consist of a fair and balanced representation of interested stakeholders, including State and local governments, tribes, recreational users, local business owners, and private landowners.

In recognition of the importance of tribal participation to the care and management of the objects identified above, and to ensure that management decisions affecting the monument reflect tribal expertise and traditional and historical knowledge, a Bears Ears Commission (Commission) is hereby established to provide guidance and recommendations on the development and implementation of management plans and on management of the monument. The Commission shall consist of one elected officer each from the Hopi Nation, Navajo Nation, Ute Mountain Ute Tribe, Ute Indian Tribe of the Uintah Ouray, and Zuni Tribe, designated by the officers' respective tribes. The Commission may adopt such procedures as it deems necessary to govern its activities, so that it may effectively partner with the Federal agencies by making continuing contributions to inform decisions regarding the management of the monument.

The Secretaries shall meaningfully engage the Commission or, should the Commission no longer exist, the tribal governments through some other entity composed of elected tribal government officers (comparable entity), in the development of the management plan and to inform subsequent management of the monument. To that end, in developing or revising the management plan, the Secretaries shall carefully and fully consider integrating the traditional and historical knowledge and special expertise of the Commission or comparable entity. If the Secretaries decide not to incorporate specific recommendations submitted to them in writing by the Commission or comparable entity, they will provide the Commission or comparable entity with a written explanation of their reasoning. The management plan shall also set forth parameters for continued meaningful engagement with the Commission or comparable entity in implementation of the management plan.

To further the protective purposes of the monument, the Secretary of the Interior shall explore entering into a memorandum of understanding with the State that would set forth terms, pursuant to applicable laws and regulations, for an exchange of land currently owned by the State of Utah and administered by the Utah School and Institutional Trust Lands Administration within the boundary of the monument for land of approximately equal value managed by the BLM outside the boundary of the monument. The Secretary of the Interior shall report to the President by January 19, 2017, regarding the potential for such an exchange.

Nothing in this proclamation shall be deemed to enlarge or diminish the rights or jurisdiction of any Indian tribe. The Secretaries shall, to the maximum extent permitted by law and in consultation with Indian tribes, ensure the protection of Indian sacred sites and traditional cultural properties in the monument and provide access by members of Indian tribes for traditional cultural and customary uses, consistent with the American Indian Religious Freedom Act (42 U.S.C. 1996) and Executive Order 13007 of May 24, 1996 (Indian Sacred Sites), including collection of medicines, berries and other vegetation, forest products, and firewood for personal noncommercial use in a manner consistent with the care and management of the objects identified above.

For purposes of protecting and restoring the objects identified above, the Secretaries shall prepare a transportation plan that designates the roads and trails where motorized and non-motorized mechanized vehicle use will be allowed. Except for emergency or authorized administrative purposes, motorized and non-motorized mechanized vehicle use shall be allowed only on roads and trails designated for such use, consistent with the care and management of such objects. Any additional roads or trails designated for motorized vehicle use must be for the purposes of public safety or protection of such objects.

Laws, regulations, and policies followed by USFS or BLM in issuing and administering grazing permits or leases on lands under their jurisdiction shall continue to apply with regard to the lands in the monument to ensure the ongoing consistency with the care and management of the objects identified above.

Nothing in this proclamation shall be deemed to enlarge or diminish the jurisdiction of the State of Utah, including its jurisdiction and authority with respect to fish and wildlife management.

Nothing in this proclamation shall preclude low-level overflights of military aircraft, the designation of new units of special use airspace, or the use or establishment of military flight training routes over the lands reserved by this proclamation consistent with the care and management of the objects identified above.

Nothing in this proclamation shall be construed to alter the authority or responsibility of any party with respect to emergency response activities within the monument, including wildland fire response.

Nothing in this proclamation shall be deemed to revoke any existing withdrawal, reservation, or appropriation; however, the monument shall be the dominant reservation.

Warning is hereby given to all unauthorized persons not to appropriate, injure, destroy, or remove any feature of the monument and not to locate or settle upon any of the lands thereof.

IN WITNESS WHEREOF, I have hereunto set my hand this twenty-eighth day of December, in the year of our Lord two thousand sixteen, and of the Independence of the United States of America the two hundred and forty-first.

BARACK OBAMA

Zuni Pueblo and Native people across the country celebrate President Obama's proclamation of Bears Ears National Monument.

Mormon history, the Constitution and laws, and white man's history are written on paper. Our history—the Native history—is written in stone on canyon walls. We celebrate knowing our history at Bears Ears will be protected for future generations, forever."

OCTAVIUS SEOWTEWA
Zuni Cultural Resources Advisory Committee Chairman
& Zuni Medicine Society leader

As human beings we are entrusted with the responsibility to protect the environment, including Mother Earth, the air, water, sunlight, which are the basic Elements of life. The abundance of Mother Earth's resources are becoming scarce today and the encroachment on Mother Earth is becoming more fierce. The natural beauty of Mother Earth is at stake and because of this our responsibility to care for and preserve what is left is of the utmost importance.

This is why designating Bears Ears as a national monument is crucial. Like the spirit of our ancestors at Bears Ears, we want our future generations to see and enjoy the natural beauty of Mother Earth. These are the reasons why we extend tremendous gratitude to President Obama for designating Bears Ears as a national monument and honoring Mother Earth and her spirit to thrive."

MARK MARYBOY
former San Juan County Commissioner
& Utah's first Native American elected official,
former Navajo Nation Council Delegate

map created by
STEPHANIE SMITH

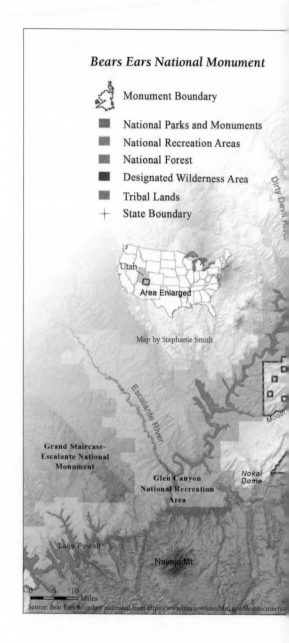

Bears Ears National Monument

Monument Boundary

National Parks and Monuments
National Recreation Areas
National Forest
Designated Wilderness Area
Tribal Lands
State Boundary

Utah

Area Enlarged

Map by Stephanie Smith

Dirty Devil Arm

Escalante River

Moqu

Grand Staircase-
Escalante National
Monument

Glen Canyon
National Recreation
Area

Nokai
Dome

Lake Powell

Navajo Mt.

0   5   10
Miles

Source: Bear Ears boundary estimated from https://www.blm.gov/sites/blm.gov/files/documents

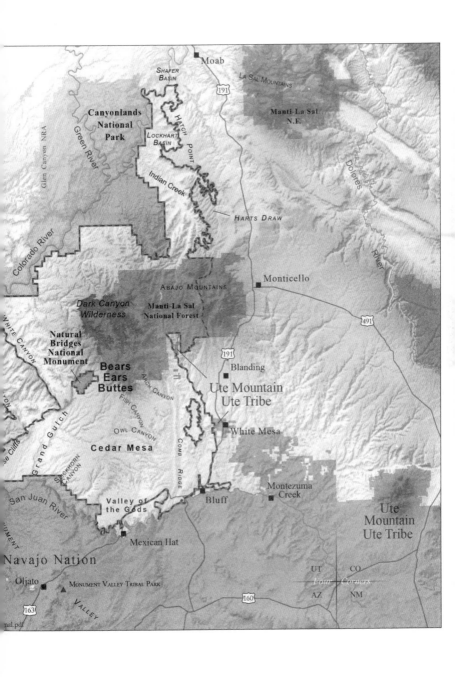

Moab

SHAFER
BASIN

LA SAL MOUNTAINS

191

Manti-La Sal
N.F.

**Canyonlands
National
Park**

Glen Canyon NRA

Green River

HATCH POINT

LOCKHART
BASIN

Indian Creek

Dolores River

HARTS DRAW

Colorado River

ABAJO MOUNTAINS

Monticello

491

*Dark Canyon
Wilderness*

**Manti-La Sal
National Forest**

WHITE CANYON

**Natural
Bridges
National
Monument**

191

Blanding

**Bears
Ears
Buttes**

ARCH CANYON

Ute Mountain
Ute Tribe

FISH CANYON

White Mesa

OWL CANYON

Cedar Mesa

COMB RIDGE

Grand Gulch

Montezuma
Creek

STICKHORN CANYON

**Ute
Mountain
Ute Tribe**

San Juan River

Valley of
the Gods

Bluff

Mexican Hat

UT   CO

Navajo Nation

Oljato

MONUMENT VALLEY TRIBAL PARK

Four Corners

AZ   NM

163

VALLEY

160

nal.pdf

TORREY HOUSE PRESS
VOICES FOR THE LAND

The economy is a wholly owned subsidiary of the environment,
not the other way around.

SENATOR GAYLORD NELSON
founder of Earth Day

Torrey House Press is an independent nonprofit publisher
promoting environmental conservation through literature.
We believe that culture is changed through conversation
and that lively, contemporary literature is the cutting edge of
social change. We strive to identify exceptional writers, nur-
ture their work, and engage the widest possible audience;
to publish diverse voices with transformative stories that
illuminate important facets of our ever-changing planet; to
develop literary resources for the conservation movement,
educating and entertaining readers, inspiring action.

Visit www.torreyhouse.org for reading group discussion
guides, author interviews, and more.